KETOVORE D

COOKBOOK

A Beginners guide with Carnivore-Inspired Ketogenic Recipes and Diet Meal Plan with

Full-Color Pictures"

Jim amos

TABLE OF CONTENT

INTRODUCTION

Welcome to the Ketovore Diet Cookbook, where the world of ketogenic and carnivore diets come together in a culinary adventure designed to satisfy both your nutritional needs and your taste buds. Whether you're a seasoned low-carb enthusiast or new to the world of ketogenic eating, this cookbook is your guide to achieving optimal health through a balanced, high-fat, and low-carb lifestyle.

The ketovore diet is a fusion of the popular keto and carnivore diets, emphasizing nutrient-dense animal-based foods while maintaining the metabolic benefits of ketosis. By focusing on whole, unprocessed ingredients and reducing carbohydrates, the ketovore diet offers a sustainable approach to weight management, enhanced mental clarity, and increased energy levels.

In this cookbook, you'll discover a diverse collection of recipes that prioritize quality proteins and healthy fats. From succulent meats and savory seafood to nourishing soups and delectable desserts, each recipe is crafted to keep you in ketosis while providing all the essential nutrients your body craves. You'll find inspiration for every meal of the day, ensuring that your journey on the ketovore path is both enjoyable and sustainable.

In addition to delicious recipes, you'll learn about the science behind the ketovore diet and gain valuable tips for transitioning to this lifestyle. Whether you're seeking weight loss, improved health markers, or simply a new way to enjoy food, the ketovore diet offers a flexible and satisfying solution.

Embark on this journey with us, and let the Ketovore Diet Cookbook become your trusted companion as you explore the delicious possibilities of a low-carb, high-protein lifestyle. Together, let's savor the joys of eating well while embracing the transformative power of food.

CHAPTER 1

WHAT IS THE KETOVORE DIET?

Welcome to the world of the Ketovore Diet, a fascinating blend of ketogenic and carnivorous eating styles that has captured the interest of health enthusiasts and foodies alike.

The Ketovore Diet is essentially a hybrid approach that combines the principles of the ketogenic diet, which emphasizes low carbohydrate intake and high fat consumption, with the carnivore diet, which is all about eating animal-based foods. This dietary approach offers a unique and flexible way to enjoy the benefits of both diets, focusing on whole, nutrient-dense foods while minimizing carbohydrates.

The Basics of the Ketovore Diet

At its core, the Ketovore Diet encourages the consumption of high-quality animal proteins and fats, such as beef, pork, lamb, poultry, fish, and eggs, while reducing or eliminating carbohydrate-rich foods. The primary goal is to enter and maintain a state of ketosis, where the body burns fat for fuel instead of carbohydrates. This metabolic state is achieved by significantly lowering carb intake, which helps the body shift its energy source from glucose to fat.

In addition to animal-based foods, the Ketovore Diet allows for moderate consumption of low-carb vegetables, such as leafy greens and cruciferous vegetables, as well as healthy fats like olive oil, avocado oil, and butter. Some individuals also include small amounts of nuts, seeds, and dairy products, depending on their personal preferences and dietary goals.

How the Ketovore Diet Works

The Ketovore Diet works by reducing insulin levels and promoting the production of ketones, which are molecules produced by the liver when fat is broken down.

Ketones serve as an alternative energy source for the brain and muscles, providing sustained energy and mental clarity. By minimizing carbohydrate intake and increasing fat consumption, the Ketovore Diet helps stabilize blood sugar levels, reduce hunger, and enhance fat loss.

This approach is particularly appealing to those who have tried traditional ketogenic diets but seek a more simplified and sustainable eating pattern. The focus on nutrient-dense animal foods ensures that followers of the Ketovore Diet receive essential vitamins and minerals, such as B vitamins, iron, zinc, and omega-3 fatty acids, which are crucial for overall health and well-being.

Benefits of the Ketovore Diet

The Ketovore Diet offers a range of benefits that can contribute to improved health and vitality. Let's explore some of the key advantages of this dietary approach:

Enhanced Weight Loss and Metabolic Health

One of the most significant benefits of the Ketovore Diet is its potential for weight loss and improved metabolic health. By reducing carbohydrate intake and focusing on high-quality fats and proteins, the diet helps promote satiety and reduce overall calorie consumption. This, in turn, can lead to weight loss, particularly in individuals who struggle with insulin resistance or metabolic syndrome.

Moreover, the Ketovore Diet can help regulate hormones involved in appetite control, such as leptin and ghrelin, making it easier for individuals to maintain a healthy weight. The diet's emphasis on whole, unprocessed foods also supports optimal digestion and nutrient absorption, further enhancing metabolic health.

Increased Energy Levels and Mental Clarity

Many followers of the Ketovore Diet report increased energy levels and improved mental clarity, thanks to the diet's ability to stabilize blood sugar levels and provide a steady supply of energy. Unlike high-carbohydrate diets that can cause energy crashes and brain fog, the Ketovore Diet relies on fats and ketones as a consistent energy source.

Ketones are known to have neuroprotective effects, which can enhance cognitive function and focus. This makes the Ketovore Diet particularly appealing to individuals who seek improved mental performance and sustained energy throughout the day.

Reduced Inflammation and Improved Immune Function

The Ketovore Diet's emphasis on anti-inflammatory foods, such as omega-3-rich fish and grass-fed meats, can help reduce inflammation and support immune function. Chronic inflammation is linked to various health issues, including autoimmune diseases, heart disease, and certain cancers.

By minimizing processed foods and sugars, the Ketovore Diet helps lower inflammatory markers and promotes a healthier immune response.

Additionally, the diet's focus on nutrient-dense foods ensures that individuals receive essential vitamins and minerals that support immune health, such as vitamin D, zinc, and selenium. This can lead to improved resilience against infections and a reduced risk of chronic diseases.

Better Blood Sugar Control and Insulin Sensitivity

For individuals with insulin resistance or type 2 diabetes, the Ketovore Diet can be a powerful tool for improving blood sugar control and insulin sensitivity. By limiting carbohydrate intake, the diet helps reduce the need for insulin and stabilizes blood glucose levels. This can lead to improved glycemic control and a reduced risk of diabetes-related complications.

Furthermore, the Ketovore Diet's emphasis on whole, unprocessed foods helps prevent the blood sugar spikes and crashes associated with refined carbohydrates, leading to more stable energy levels and improved overall health.

Simplified Eating and Improved Food Quality

One of the most appealing aspects of the Ketovore Diet is its simplicity and focus on food quality. By prioritizing whole, nutrient-dense animal foods, individuals can enjoy a straightforward and satisfying eating pattern without the need for complex meal planning or calorie counting.

The diet encourages mindful eating and a greater appreciation for the flavors and textures of real, unprocessed foods. This can lead to a more positive relationship with food and a greater awareness of the body's hunger and satiety cues.

Foods to Embrace

Meat and Poultry

The foundation of the Ketovore diet is high-quality meat and poultry. Grass-fed beef, pasture-raised chicken, lamb, pork, and turkey are excellent sources of protein and essential fats. These meats provide vital nutrients like B vitamins, iron, and zinc, which are crucial for maintaining energy levels and supporting a robust immune system.

- **Grass-Fed Beef**: Rich in omega-3 fatty acids and conjugated linoleic acid (CLA), which can support heart health and reduce inflammation.
- **Pork**: Offers a good balance of protein and healthy fats, especially when sourced from pasture-raised animals.
- **Chicken and Turkey**: Lean options that are versatile and packed with B vitamins.

Fish and Seafood

Incorporating fish and seafood is a great way to boost your intake of omega-3 fatty acids, essential for brain health and reducing inflammation. Opt for fatty fish like salmon, mackerel, sardines, and anchovies, which are high in healthy fats and low in carbohydrates.

- **Salmon:** Packed with omega-3s, vitamin D, and selenium, contributing to brain and heart health.
- **Mackerel:** A rich source of healthy fats and vitamin B12, supporting energy production and neurological function.
- **Shellfish:** Clams, mussels, and oysters provide zinc and other minerals that support immune function.

Animal Fats

Healthy fats are a cornerstone of the Ketovore diet. Embrace animal-based fats like tallow, lard, and duck fat, which are excellent for cooking and provide sustained energy. Butter and ghee, especially when sourced from grass-fed cows, are also valuable additions.

- **Tallow and Lard:** Rendered animal fats that are stable for cooking and add flavor to meals.
- **Butter and Ghee:** Rich in butyrate, a short-chain fatty acid beneficial for gut health.

Organ Meats

Organ meats, often called nature's multivitamins, are packed with nutrients that are hard to find elsewhere. Liver, heart, kidneys, and brain are rich in vitamins A, D, E, K, and minerals like iron and copper.

- **Liver:** High in vitamin A, supporting vision, skin health, and immune function.
- **Heart:** Contains CoQ10, which supports heart health and cellular energy production.

Eggs

Eggs are a versatile and nutrient-dense food, rich in high-quality protein, healthy fats, and essential nutrients like choline and vitamin D. They are an excellent choice for breakfast or any meal.

- **Choline:** Supports brain health and cognitive function.
- **Vitamin D:** Crucial for bone health and immune support.

Foods to Avoid

Sugary Foods and Drinks

To maintain ketosis and reap the benefits of the Ketovore diet, it's essential to avoid sugar and sugary drinks. These include soft drinks, fruit juices, candy, pastries, and anything with added sugars.

- **Soft Drinks and Fruit Juices:** High in sugar and can spike insulin levels, leading to energy crashes and weight gain.
- **Candy and Pastries:** Empty calories that provide no nutritional benefit and disrupt ketosis.

Grains and Starches

Grains and starchy foods like bread, pasta, rice, and potatoes are high in carbohydrates, making them incompatible with the Ketovore lifestyle. Eliminating these foods helps maintain low insulin levels and supports fat burning.

- **Bread and Pasta**: High in carbohydrates and can cause blood sugar spikes.
- **Rice and Potatoes**: Convert to sugar in the body, hindering ketosis.

Legumes

Beans, lentils, and peas are not only high in carbohydrates but also contain antinutrients like lectins and phytic acid, which can interfere with nutrient absorption.

- **Beans and Lentils**: High in carbs and can cause digestive discomfort for some people.
- **Peas**: Though lower in carbs than other legumes, they still contain enough to disrupt ketosis.

Processed Foods

Processed foods are often loaded with unhealthy additives, preservatives, and hidden sugars. They can also contain unhealthy fats and lack the nutritional benefits of whole, natural foods.

- **Packaged Snacks**: Often high in carbs and unhealthy fats.
- **Ready Meals**: Contain preservatives and hidden sugars that can affect health and ketosis.

Vegetable Oils

Oils like canola, soybean, corn, and sunflower are high in omega-6 fatty acids, which can promote inflammation and disrupt the balance of omega-3s in the diet. Opt for animal-based fats and natural oils like olive oil instead.

- **Canola and Soybean Oil**: Processed oils that can lead to inflammation.
- **Corn and Sunflower Oil**: High in omega-6 fatty acids, which can disrupt the balance of healthy fats.

Tips for a Successful Transition

Gradual Transition

Transitioning to a Ketovore lifestyle doesn't have to happen overnight. Gradually reduce your carbohydrate intake and replace it with nutrient-dense animal foods. This helps your body adapt to burning fat for fuel and minimizes the initial discomfort sometimes associated with low-carb diets.

Listen to Your Body

Pay attention to how your body responds to different foods. Some people may thrive on a strict Ketovore diet, while others might need to incorporate a small amount of low-carb vegetables or dairy. Customize the diet to suit your individual needs and preferences.

Stay Hydrated

Adequate hydration is essential, especially during the initial transition when your body sheds excess water weight. Drink plenty of water and consider adding a pinch of salt to maintain electrolyte balance.

Focus on Quality

Whenever possible, choose high-quality, pasture-raised, and grass-fed animal products. These provide better nutritional profiles and support ethical and sustainable farming practices.

Monitor Your Progress

Keep track of your progress, energy levels, and overall well-being. This can help you identify what works best for you and make any necessary adjustments.

CHAPTER 2

BREAKFAST RECIPES

Savory Beef and Egg Breakfast Bowl

Serves: 1

Cooking Time: 15 minutes

Ingredients and Portions/Measurements:

- **Ground Beef (80/20 blend):** 4 oz (Rich in protein and healthy fats, providing sustained energy and supporting muscle health)
- **Eggs:** 2 large (High-quality protein source with essential amino acids, promoting satiety and metabolic health)
- **Butter (Grass-fed):** 1 tablespoon (Provides healthy fats and conjugated linoleic acid, beneficial for reducing inflammation)
- **Salt (Himalayan or Sea Salt):** 1/4 teaspoon (Trace minerals for electrolyte balance)
- **Black Pepper:** To taste (Contains piperine, which can enhance nutrient absorption)
- **Optional Garnish - Chopped Chives:** 1 tablespoon (Adds flavor and contains vitamin K and antioxidants)

Instructions:

Cook the Beef:

- Heat a non-stick skillet over medium heat. Add the ground beef and cook, stirring occasionally, until browned and cooked through, about 5-7 minutes. Season with a pinch of salt and pepper.
- Once cooked, remove the beef from the skillet and set aside, leaving the fat in the pan.

Cook the Eggs:

- In the same skillet, add butter and let it melt. Crack the eggs into the skillet and cook to your preferred level of doneness (sunny side up, over easy, etc.). Season with a pinch of salt and pepper.

Assemble the Bowl:

- Place the cooked beef in a bowl and top with the eggs. Sprinkle with chopped chives, if using.

Serve and Enjoy:

- Serve immediately, savoring the rich flavors and satisfying textures of this Ketovore breakfast bowl.

Scientific Note:

Ground Beef provides a robust source of complete protein and healthy fats essential for muscle maintenance and metabolic health. It contains vital nutrients such as iron and vitamin B12, which are important for energy production and neurological function.

Eggs are an excellent source of high-quality protein and healthy fats, including omega-3 fatty acids (especially in pasture-raised eggs). They contribute to satiety and help maintain stable blood sugar levels, which is crucial for those following a Ketovore diet.

Butter, especially from grass-fed sources, contains conjugated linoleic acid (CLA) and omega-3 fatty acids, which have anti-inflammatory properties. It also provides fat-soluble vitamins such as A, D, E, and K2.

Nutritional Information (per serving):

- Calories: ~550
- Protein: 40g
- Total Fat: 44g
- Saturated Fat: 17g
- Carbohydrates: <1g
- Fiber: 0g

Pork Belly and Egg Frittata

Serves: 1

Cooking Time: 25 minutes

Ingredients and Portions/Measurements:

- **Pork Belly (Sliced):** 4 oz (Rich in healthy fats and protein, providing energy and aiding in muscle maintenance)
- **Eggs:** 3 large (High-quality protein source with essential amino acids, supporting metabolic health)
- **Heavy Cream:** 2 tablespoons (Adds richness and fat, keeping the dish creamy and satisfying)

- **Salt (Himalayan or Sea Salt):** 1/4 teaspoon (Contains essential minerals for electrolyte balance)
- **Black Pepper:** To taste (Contains piperine, which can enhance nutrient absorption)
- **Garlic Powder:** 1/4 teaspoon (Adds flavor without carbs)
- **Optional Garnish - Fresh Parsley:** 1 tablespoon, chopped (Provides a burst of freshness and vitamins)

Instructions:

Prepare the Pork Belly:

- Preheat the oven to 375°F (190°C).
- In an oven-safe skillet over medium heat, cook the pork belly slices until crispy, about 6-8 minutes. Remove from the skillet and set aside, leaving the rendered fat in the pan.

Make the Egg Mixture:

- In a bowl, whisk together the eggs, heavy cream, salt, black pepper, and garlic powder until well combined.

Assemble the Frittata:

- Pour the egg mixture into the same skillet with the pork fat. Stir gently to combine the fat with the eggs.

- Add the cooked pork belly back into the skillet, spreading it evenly throughout the egg mixture.

Cook the Frittata:

- Transfer the skillet to the preheated oven and bake for 12-15 minutes or until the frittata is set and lightly golden on top.

Serve:

- Remove from the oven and let it cool slightly. Sprinkle with chopped parsley if desired.
- Slice and serve warm.

Scientific Note:

Pork Belly is an excellent source of fat and protein, vital for those on a Ketovore diet. It provides energy and essential fatty acids, supporting metabolic functions and satiety.

Eggs deliver high-quality protein and essential nutrients, including choline, which aids in brain function and liver health. The inclusion of heavy cream enhances the fat content, aligning with the high-fat requirements of the Ketovore diet.

Heavy Cream adds a creamy texture and additional fats, crucial for maintaining ketosis and providing a satisfying, energy-dense meal.

Nutritional Information (per serving):

- Calories: ~600

- Protein: 36g
- Total Fat: 52g
- Saturated Fat: 20g
- Carbohydrates: <1g
- Fiber: 0g

Cheesy Beef Omelette Roll

Serves: 1

Cooking Time: 20 minutes

Ingredients and Portions/Measurements:

- Ground Beef: 3 oz (A rich source of protein and essential nutrients like iron and B vitamins)
- Eggs: 2 large (Provide high-quality protein and important fats for energy and brain health)
- Cheddar Cheese (Shredded): 1/4 cup (Adds flavor and healthy fats, helping maintain ketosis)
- Butter: 1 tablespoon (Provides saturated fats needed for a ketogenic diet)
- Salt (Himalayan or Sea Salt): 1/4 teaspoon (Contains trace minerals important for hydration and nerve function)
- Black Pepper: To taste (Enhances flavor without adding carbs)
- Onion Powder: 1/4 teaspoon (For flavor enhancement without carbs)
- Paprika: 1/4 teaspoon (Adds a hint of smokiness)

Instructions:

Cook the Beef:

- In a non-stick skillet over medium heat, add butter and let it melt. Add the ground beef, seasoning it with salt, pepper, onion powder, and paprika. Cook until browned, about 5-7 minutes. Remove from the skillet and set aside.

Prepare the Omelette:

- In a bowl, whisk the eggs until smooth. Pour into the same skillet over medium heat, swirling to spread evenly. Allow it to cook until the edges start to set.

Add Cheese and Beef:

- Sprinkle the shredded cheddar cheese over one half of the omelette. Add the cooked beef on top of the cheese.

Roll the Omelette:

- Carefully roll the omelette from the cheese side to form a roll, ensuring the cheese melts inside.

Serve:

- Once the omelette is cooked through, transfer to a plate, and let it cool for a minute before slicing.

Scientific Note:

Ground Beef provides not only protein but also conjugated linoleic acid (CLA), which has been shown to support fat metabolism and reduce inflammation.

Eggs are nutrient-dense, offering essential fats and vitamins such as choline, which plays a role in liver function and cognitive health.

Cheddar Cheese provides calcium and additional fats that are beneficial for maintaining ketosis and supporting bone health.

Nutritional Information (per serving):

- Calories: ~480
- Protein: 36g
- Total Fat: 38g
- Saturated Fat: 18g
- Carbohydrates: <1g

- Fiber: 0g

Lamb and Egg Breakfast Skillet

Serves: 1

Cooking Time: 25 minutes

Ingredients and Portions/Measurements:

- **Ground Lamb:** 4 oz (Provides rich protein and healthy fats, including omega-3 fatty acids)
- **Eggs:** 2 large (Offer high-quality protein and essential fats)
- **Ghee:** 1 tablespoon (Clarified butter that adds flavor and healthy fats)
- **Zucchini:** 1/4 cup, diced (A low-carb vegetable providing vitamins and fiber)
- **Salt (Himalayan or Sea Salt):** 1/4 teaspoon (Rich in trace minerals, supporting electrolyte balance)

- **Black Pepper**: To taste (Enhances flavor and aids digestion)
- **Cumin Powder**: 1/4 teaspoon (Adds warmth and supports digestion)
- **Fresh Thyme**: 1 teaspoon, chopped (Optional garnish for flavor and antioxidants)

Instructions:

Prepare the Lamb:

- Heat a non-stick skillet over medium heat and add the ghee.
- Add the ground lamb, seasoning with salt, pepper, and cumin powder. Cook until browned, about 7-10 minutes. Remove from the skillet and set aside.

Cook the Zucchini:

- In the same skillet, add the diced zucchini and sauté for 3-4 minutes until slightly softened.

Cook the Eggs:

- Create a space in the skillet and crack the eggs into the space. Cook them to your preferred doneness, seasoning with a pinch of salt and pepper.

Combine and Serve:

- Add the cooked lamb back to the skillet and gently mix with the zucchini. Let everything heat through for an additional 2 minutes.
- Garnish with fresh thyme if desired, and serve immediately.

Scientific Note:

Lamb is a nutrient-dense source of protein and contains healthy fats that support ketosis. It's rich in omega-3 fatty acids, which are anti-inflammatory and beneficial for heart health.

Eggs are an excellent source of essential amino acids and fats, aiding in satiety and maintaining energy levels throughout the day.

Ghee provides medium-chain triglycerides (MCTs), which are easily absorbed and utilized for energy, promoting ketosis and supporting metabolic health.

Nutritional Information (per serving):

- Calories: ~520
- Protein: 40g
- Total Fat: 42g
- Saturated Fat: 18g
- Carbohydrates: 2g
- Fiber: 0g

Chicken Liver Pâté Breakfast Cups

Serves: 1

Cooking Time: 30 minutes

Ingredients and Portions/Measurements:

- **Chicken Livers**: 4 oz (Rich in iron, vitamin A, and essential amino acids, supporting energy and immune function)
- **Duck Fat**: 2 tablespoons (Provides healthy fats and adds a rich flavor)
- **Eggs**: 2 large (High-quality protein and healthy fats)
- **Onion Powder**: 1/4 teaspoon (For flavor without carbs)
- **Salt (Himalayan or Sea Salt)**: 1/4 teaspoon (Provides trace minerals)
- **Black Pepper**: To taste (Enhances flavor)
- **Fresh Sage**: 1 teaspoon, chopped (Adds a hint of earthiness and aids digestion)
- **Optional - Spinach Leaves**: 1/4 cup (Provides vitamins and minerals)

Instructions:

Prepare the Chicken Livers:

- Rinse the chicken livers under cold water and pat them dry with a paper towel.
- In a skillet over medium heat, melt 1 tablespoon of duck fat. Add the chicken livers and cook for 5-7 minutes until browned on the outside and slightly pink inside. Season with salt, pepper, and onion powder.

Blend the Pâté:

- Transfer the cooked chicken livers to a food processor. Add the remaining duck fat and fresh sage. Blend until smooth and creamy.

Cook the Eggs:

- In a separate skillet, melt a small amount of duck fat over medium heat. Crack the eggs into the skillet and cook to your preferred doneness (scrambled or sunny-side-up).

Assemble the Breakfast Cups:

- If using spinach, lightly sauté the spinach leaves in the same skillet used for the eggs until just wilted.

- Place the sautéed spinach in a serving cup or bowl. Top with the chicken liver pâté and cooked eggs.

Serve:

- Garnish with additional fresh sage if desired and serve immediately.

Scientific Note:

Chicken Livers are nutrient-dense, providing a rich source of vitamins and minerals such as vitamin A, iron, and B vitamins, which support energy production and immune health.

Duck Fat is a healthy source of monounsaturated fats, which can support heart health and provide a steady source of energy, aiding in ketosis.

Eggs are an excellent source of protein and healthy fats, contributing to satiety and maintaining stable energy levels.

Nutritional Information (per serving):

- Calories: ~450
- Protein: 35g
- Total Fat: 35g
- Saturated Fat: 12g
- Carbohydrates: 1g

Pork and Egg Breakfast Tacos

Serves: 1

Cooking Time: 20 minutes

Ingredients and Portions/Measurements:

- **Pork Shoulder (Thinly Sliced):** 4 oz (High in protein and healthy fats, providing energy and supporting muscle maintenance)
- **Eggs:** 2 large (High-quality protein and essential fats for energy and satiety)
- **Pork Rind Crumbs:** 1/4 cup (Low-carb alternative for taco shells)
- **Butter:** 1 tablespoon (Adds healthy fats and flavor)
- **Salt (Himalayan or Sea Salt):** 1/4 teaspoon (Contains trace minerals for electrolyte balance)
- **Black Pepper:** To taste (Enhances flavor)
- **Cumin:** 1/4 teaspoon (Adds warmth and supports digestion)

- **Fresh Cilantro:** 1 tablespoon, chopped (Optional garnish for freshness and vitamins)

Instructions:

Prepare the Pork:

- Season the pork slices with salt, pepper, and cumin.
- Heat a skillet over medium heat and add butter. Once melted, add the pork slices and cook until browned and cooked through, about 5-7 minutes. Remove from the skillet and set aside.

Prepare the Pork Rind Taco Shells:

- While the pork is cooking, preheat the oven to 350°F (175°C).
- Form small taco shells with the pork rind crumbs by pressing them into muffin tins or onto a baking sheet lined with parchment paper.
- Bake for 5-7 minutes until they become crisp and hold their shape.

Cook the Eggs:

- In the same skillet, crack the eggs and cook them to your preferred doneness (scrambled or fried). Season with a pinch of salt and pepper.

Assemble the Tacos:

- Place the cooked pork slices into the pork rind taco shells.
- Top with cooked eggs and garnish with chopped cilantro, if desired.

Serve:

- Serve immediately and enjoy the flavorful combination of pork and eggs in a low-carb taco shell.

Scientific Note:

Pork Shoulder is rich in protein and healthy fats, which are essential for muscle maintenance and energy on a Ketovore diet. It provides B vitamins, which are important for energy metabolism.

Pork Rind Crumbs offer a crunchy, low-carb alternative to traditional taco shells, making them ideal for maintaining ketosis.

Eggs are a complete protein source, providing essential amino acids and fats, which support brain health and satiety.

Nutritional Information (per serving):

- Calories: ~520
- Protein: 44g
- Total Fat: 40g
- Saturated Fat: 16g
- Carbohydrates: <1g
- Fiber: 0g

Bacon-Wrapped Scallop Omelette

Serves: 1

Cooking Time: 20 minutes

Ingredients and Portions/Measurements:

- Scallops: 3 large (High in protein and low in carbohydrates, rich in selenium and B12)
- Bacon Strips: 3 (Provides healthy fats and adds a savory flavor)
- Eggs: 2 large (Offers high-quality protein and essential fats)
- Ghee: 1 tablespoon (Provides healthy fats and a rich flavor)
- Salt (Himalayan or Sea Salt): 1/4 teaspoon (Contains trace minerals)
- Black Pepper: To taste (Enhances flavor)
- Dill: 1 teaspoon, chopped (Optional garnish for added flavor)

Instructions:

Wrap the Scallops:

- Wrap each scallop with a strip of bacon and secure with a toothpick.

Cook the Bacon-Wrapped Scallops:

- Heat a skillet over medium heat and add the ghee.
- Place the bacon-wrapped scallops in the skillet and cook for 3-4 minutes on each side until the bacon is crispy and the scallops are cooked through. Remove from the skillet and set aside.

Prepare the Omelette:

- In a bowl, whisk the eggs with salt and pepper.
- Pour the eggs into the same skillet over medium heat, swirling to spread evenly. Cook until the edges start to set.

Assemble the Omelette:

- Place the bacon-wrapped scallops on one side of the omelette.
- Fold the omelette over to cover the scallops and cook for an additional 1-2 minutes until the omelette is set.

Serve:

- Transfer the omelette to a plate and garnish with chopped dill if desired. Serve immediately.

Scientific Note:

Scallops are an excellent source of lean protein and provide essential nutrients like selenium, which supports immune function, and vitamin B12, which is important for nerve health.

Bacon adds flavor and healthy fats, which are crucial for maintaining ketosis. The combination of protein and fat helps keep you satiated.

Eggs are nutrient-dense, offering essential amino acids and fats that promote satiety and energy stability.

Nutritional Information (per serving):

- Calories: ~450
- Protein: 35g
- Total Fat: 36g
- Saturated Fat: 14g
- Cholesterol: 470mg
- Carbohydrates: <1g
- Fiber: 0g

Venison Sausage and Mushroom Scramble

Serves: 1

Cooking Time: 20 minutes

Ingredients and Portions/Measurements:

- **Venison Sausage:** 4 oz (Lean protein source rich in iron and B vitamins)
- **Eggs:** 2 large (Provides high-quality protein and healthy fats)
- **Cremini Mushrooms:** 1/4 cup, sliced (Low in carbs and high in antioxidants)
- **Butter:** 1 tablespoon (Adds flavor and healthy fats)
- **Salt (Himalayan or Sea Salt):** 1/4 teaspoon (Contains essential trace minerals)
- **Black Pepper:** To taste (Enhances flavor)
- **Chives:** 1 tablespoon, chopped (Optional garnish for added flavor and nutrients)

Instructions:

Cook the Sausage:

- In a skillet over medium heat, melt the butter. Add the venison sausage and cook until browned and cooked through, about 5-7 minutes. Remove from the skillet and set aside.

Sauté the Mushrooms:

- In the same skillet, add the sliced mushrooms and sauté until golden and tender, about 3-4 minutes.

Prepare the Scramble:

- In a bowl, whisk the eggs with salt and pepper.
- Pour the eggs into the skillet with the mushrooms and cook, stirring gently, until the eggs are just set.

Combine and Serve:

- Add the cooked venison sausage back into the skillet and mix with the eggs and mushrooms.
- Garnish with chopped chives if desired, and serve immediately.

Scientific Note:

Venison Sausage is a lean source of protein that is lower in fat than traditional pork sausage, making it a great choice for a Ketovore diet. It provides essential nutrients such as iron, which supports oxygen transport in the body.

Mushrooms are low in carbohydrates and high in antioxidants, which can help reduce inflammation and support overall health.

Eggs provide essential amino acids and fats, contributing to satiety and stable energy levels.

Nutritional Information (per serving):

- Calories: ~460
- Protein: 38g
- Total Fat: 34g
- Saturated Fat: 13g
- Carbohydrates: 2g
- Fiber: 1g

Duck Confit and Egg Breakfast Hash

Serves: 1

Cooking Time: 30 minutes

Ingredients and Portions/Measurements:

- Duck Confit: 4 oz (Rich in healthy fats and high-quality protein)
- Eggs: 2 large (Provide essential amino acids and healthy fats)
- Cauliflower: 1/2 cup, riced (Low in carbs, provides fiber and vitamin C)
- Duck Fat: 1 tablespoon (Enhances flavor and provides healthy fats)
- Salt (Himalayan or Sea Salt): 1/4 teaspoon (Contains trace minerals for electrolyte balance)
- Black Pepper: To taste (Enhances flavor)
- Rosemary: 1/2 teaspoon, chopped (Adds flavor and has antioxidant properties)

Instructions:

Prepare the Cauliflower Rice:

- In a skillet over medium heat, melt the duck fat. Add the riced cauliflower and cook until tender, about 5 minutes. Season with salt, pepper, and rosemary.

Cook the Duck Confit:

- Shred the duck confit into bite-sized pieces and add to the skillet with the cauliflower. Cook for 3-4 minutes until heated through and slightly crispy.

Cook the Eggs:

- In a separate skillet, cook the eggs to your preferred doneness (scrambled, sunny-side-up, etc.). Season with salt and pepper.

Assemble the Breakfast Hash:

- Place the cauliflower and duck mixture on a plate and top with the cooked eggs.

Serve:

- Garnish with additional rosemary if desired, and serve immediately.

Scientific Note:

Duck Confit is a rich source of healthy fats, particularly monounsaturated fats, which support heart health and provide a steady source of energy for those following a Ketovore diet.

Cauliflower Rice is a low-carb alternative to traditional grains, offering fiber and essential nutrients while keeping the carbohydrate content minimal.

Duck Fat is an excellent source of monounsaturated fats and adds a rich flavor to dishes, supporting ketosis and providing energy.

Nutritional Information (per serving):

- Calories: ~550
- Protein: 42g
- Total Fat: 40g
- Saturated Fat: 14g
- Carbohydrates: 3g

- Fiber: 1g

Smoked Salmon and Avocado Breakfast Boats

Serves: 1

Cooking Time: 15 minutes

Ingredients and Portions/Measurements:

- **Smoked Salmon:** 3 oz (Rich in omega-3 fatty acids and high-quality protein)
- **Avocado:** 1 small (High in healthy monounsaturated fats and fiber)
- **Eggs:** 2 large (Provides essential amino acids and healthy fats)
- **Lemon Juice:** 1 tablespoon (Adds freshness and vitamin C)
- **Olive Oil:** 1 teaspoon (Enhances flavor and adds healthy fats)
- **Salt (Himalayan or Sea Salt):** 1/4 teaspoon (Contains trace minerals)
- **Black Pepper:** To taste (Enhances flavor)

- **Dill:** 1 teaspoon, chopped (Optional garnish for added flavor and nutrients)

Instructions:

Prepare the Avocado:

- Cut the avocado in half and remove the pit. Scoop out some of the flesh to create a larger cavity, and mash it with lemon juice, olive oil, salt, and pepper.

Cook the Eggs:

- In a skillet, cook the eggs to your preferred doneness (scrambled, sunny-side-up, etc.). Season with salt and pepper.

Assemble the Breakfast Boats:

- Fill each avocado half with mashed avocado mixture. Top with smoked salmon and the cooked eggs.

Serve:

- Garnish with chopped dill if desired, and serve immediately.

Scientific Note:

Smoked Salmon is an excellent source of omega-3 fatty acids, which support brain health and reduce inflammation. It provides high-quality protein that aids in muscle maintenance and satiety.

Avocado is rich in monounsaturated fats and fiber, promoting heart health and aiding in digestion. It is low in carbohydrates, making it ideal for maintaining ketosis.

Eggs offer a complete protein profile and healthy fats, contributing to energy stability and satiety throughout the day.

Nutritional Information (per serving):

- Calories: ~500
- Protein: 35g
- Total Fat: 40g
- Saturated Fat: 10g
- Carbohydrates: 8g
- Fiber: 7g

CHAPTER 3

LUNCH RECIPES

Crispy Duck Breast with Herbed Butter

Serves: 1

Cooking Time: 30 minutes

Ingredients and Portions/Measurements:

- **Duck Breast (Skin On):** 6 oz (Rich in healthy fats and high-quality protein)
- **Butter (Grass-fed):** 2 tablespoons (Adds healthy fats and flavor)
- **Salt (Himalayan or Sea Salt):** 1/4 teaspoon (Contains essential trace minerals)
- **Black Pepper:** To taste (Enhances flavor)
- **Garlic Powder:** 1/4 teaspoon (For flavor without carbs)

- **Fresh Thyme:** 1 teaspoon, chopped (Optional garnish for added flavor and nutrients)

Instructions:

Prepare the Duck Breast:

- Preheat your oven to 400°F (200°C).
- Score the skin of the duck breast in a crosshatch pattern without cutting into the meat. Season both sides with salt, pepper, and garlic powder.

Cook the Duck Breast:

- Heat a dry, oven-safe skillet over medium-high heat. Place the duck breast skin-side down and cook until the skin is crispy and golden brown, about 6-8 minutes. Flip the duck breast and cook for an additional 2 minutes.
- Transfer the skillet to the oven and roast for 8-10 minutes, or until the duck reaches your preferred level of doneness.

Make the Herbed Butter:

- While the duck is roasting, melt the butter in a small saucepan over low heat. Add the chopped thyme and stir to combine.

Finish and Serve:

- Remove the duck breast from the oven and let it rest for a few minutes before slicing.
- Drizzle the herbed butter over the sliced duck breast and garnish with additional thyme if desired. Serve immediately.

Scientific Note:

Duck Breast is an excellent source of healthy fats and protein, which are essential for maintaining energy and muscle health on a Ketovore diet. The skin provides monounsaturated fats that support heart health and promote satiety.

Butter from grass-fed sources is rich in conjugated linoleic acid (CLA) and omega-3 fatty acids, which have anti-inflammatory properties. It also contains fat-soluble vitamins such as A, D, E, and K2.

Thyme is a flavorful herb that offers antioxidants and can support digestion and overall health.

Nutritional Information (per serving):

- Calories: ~650
- Protein: 45g
- Total Fat: 54g
- Saturated Fat: 24g
- Carbohydrates: 0g
- Fiber: 0g

Bison Ribeye Steak with Bone Marrow Butter

Serves: 1

Cooking Time: 30 minutes

Ingredients and Portions/Measurements:

- **Bison Ribeye Steak:** 8 oz (High-quality protein source, rich in iron and omega-3 fatty acids)
- **Bone Marrow:** 2 tablespoons (Rich in healthy fats and collagen)
- **Butter (Grass-fed):** 1 tablespoon (Provides additional healthy fats and flavor)
- **Salt (Himalayan or Sea Salt):** 1/4 teaspoon (Contains trace minerals for electrolyte balance)
- **Black Pepper:** To taste (Enhances flavor)
- **Rosemary:** 1 teaspoon, chopped (Optional garnish for flavor and antioxidants)

Instructions:

Prepare the Steak:

- Season the bison ribeye steak with salt and pepper on both sides.
- Preheat a skillet over medium-high heat.

Cook the Steak:

- Add the steak to the hot skillet and cook for 4-5 minutes on each side for medium-rare, or adjust the time based on your preferred level of doneness.
- Remove the steak from the skillet and let it rest for a few minutes.

Prepare the Bone Marrow Butter:

- In a small saucepan over low heat, melt the bone marrow and butter together until well combined. Stir in the chopped rosemary.

Serve:

- Slice the bison ribeye steak and drizzle with the bone marrow butter. Garnish with additional rosemary if desired.

Scientific Note:

Bison Ribeye is an excellent source of lean protein and essential fatty acids, providing nutrients like iron, which is vital for oxygen transport and energy production. Bison meat is lower in fat and calories compared to beef, making it a nutrient-dense option for those on a Ketovore diet.

Bone Marrow is rich in collagen, which supports joint health and skin elasticity. It also provides healthy fats that aid in the absorption of fat-soluble vitamins.

Butter from grass-fed sources contains conjugated linoleic acid (CLA) and omega-3 fatty acids, both of which have anti-inflammatory properties and support heart health.

Nutritional Information (per serving):

- Calories: ~750
- Protein: 55g
- Total Fat: 60g
- Saturated Fat: 26g
- Carbohydrates: 0g
- Fiber: 0g

Grilled Quail with Creamy Mushroom Sauce

Serves: 1

Cooking Time: 25 minutes

Ingredients and Portions/Measurements:

- **Quail**: 2 whole (Rich in protein and healthy fats, providing essential nutrients)
- **Olive Oil**: 1 tablespoon (Enhances flavor and provides healthy fats)
- **Salt (Himalayan or Sea Salt)**: 1/4 teaspoon (Contains essential trace minerals)
- **Black Pepper**: To taste (Enhances flavor)
- Cremini Mushrooms: 1/2 cup, sliced (Low in carbohydrates, rich in antioxidants)
- **Heavy Cream**: 1/4 cup (Adds richness and healthy fats)
- **Garlic Powder**: 1/4 teaspoon (Adds flavor without carbs)
- **Fresh Thyme**: 1 teaspoon, chopped (Optional garnish for added flavor)

Instructions:

Prepare the Quail:

- Rub the quail with olive oil and season with salt and pepper on all sides.
- Preheat a grill or grill pan over medium-high heat.

Grill the Quail:

- Place the quail on the grill and cook for 4-5 minutes on each side or until the skin is crispy and the meat is cooked through. Remove from the grill and let rest.

Prepare the Creamy Mushroom Sauce:

- In a skillet over medium heat, add the sliced mushrooms and cook until golden and tender, about 4-5 minutes.
- Stir in the heavy cream and garlic powder. Let the sauce simmer for 2-3 minutes until slightly thickened.

Serve:

- Pour the creamy mushroom sauce over the grilled quail and garnish with chopped thyme if desired.

Scientific Note:

Quail provides a unique source of high-quality protein and healthy fats. It is rich in iron and B vitamins, which are essential for energy production and neurological health. Quail meat also contains omega-3 fatty acids, contributing to heart health and inflammation reduction.

Mushrooms are low in carbohydrates and high in antioxidants, supporting immune health and reducing inflammation. They add depth of flavor without adding carbs, making them a great addition to a Ketovore diet.

Heavy Cream adds richness to the dish, providing healthy fats that support ketosis and energy maintenance. It is an excellent source of fat-soluble vitamins, including A, D, E, and K.

Nutritional Information (per serving):

- Calories: ~600
- Protein: 50g
- Total Fat: 44g
- Saturated Fat: 16g
- Carbohydrates: 4g
- Fiber: 1g

Lamb Chop with Anchovy Herb Butter

Serves: 1

Cooking Time: 30 minutes

Ingredients and Portions/Measurements:

- **Lamb Chop:** 1 (8 oz) (Rich in high-quality protein, zinc, and B vitamins)
- **Anchovy Fillets:** 2 (Provides umami flavor and essential fatty acids)
- **Butter (Grass-fed):** 2 tablespoons (Adds healthy fats and rich flavor)
- **Salt (Himalayan or Sea Salt):** 1/4 teaspoon (Contains trace minerals)

- **Black Pepper:** To taste (Enhances flavor)
- **Garlic Powder:** 1/4 teaspoon (Adds flavor without carbs)
- **Fresh Parsley:** 1 tablespoon, chopped (Optional garnish for freshness and antioxidants)

Instructions:

Prepare the Herb Butter:

- In a small bowl, mash the anchovy fillets into a paste using a fork.
- Mix the anchovy paste with softened butter, garlic powder, and half of the chopped parsley. Set aside.

Prepare the Lamb Chop:

- Season the lamb chop with salt and pepper on both sides.
- Preheat a skillet over medium-high heat.

Cook the Lamb Chop:

- Add the lamb chop to the hot skillet and sear for 4-5 minutes on each side for medium-rare, or adjust cooking time based on your preferred level of doneness.
- Remove the lamb chop from the skillet and let it rest for a few minutes.

Serve:

- Top the lamb chop with the anchovy herb butter, allowing it to melt over the meat.
- Garnish with the remaining chopped parsley and serve immediately.

Scientific Note:

Lamb is an excellent source of high-quality protein and provides essential nutrients like zinc and B vitamins, which support immune function and energy metabolism. The healthy fats in lamb aid in maintaining ketosis and provide sustained energy.

Anchovies are rich in omega-3 fatty acids and provide a savory umami flavor. They contribute to heart health by reducing inflammation and supporting brain function.

Butter from grass-fed sources contains conjugated linoleic acid (CLA) and omega-3 fatty acids, both of which have anti-inflammatory properties and support overall health.

Nutritional Information (per serving):

- Calories: ~680
- Protein: 55g
- Total Fat: 52g
- Saturated Fat: 24g
- Carbohydrates: <1g
- Fiber: 0g

Pan-Seared Pheasant Breast with Sage Brown Butter

Serves: 1

Cooking Time: 30 minutes

Ingredients and Portions/Measurements:

- **Pheasant Breast:** 1 (6 oz) (Lean protein source, rich in B vitamins and minerals)
- **Butter (Grass-fed):** 3 tablespoons (Provides healthy fats and a rich, nutty flavor)
- **Salt (Himalayan or Sea Salt):** 1/4 teaspoon (Contains trace minerals)
- **Black Pepper:** To taste (Enhances flavor)
- **Sage Leaves:** 4-5 fresh leaves (Adds an earthy aroma and flavor)
- **Lemon Zest:** 1/2 teaspoon (Optional garnish for freshness)

Instructions:

Prepare the Pheasant:

- Season the pheasant breast with salt and pepper on both sides.
- Preheat a skillet over medium heat.

Cook the Pheasant:

- Add 1 tablespoon of butter to the skillet. Once melted and sizzling, add the pheasant breast.
- Cook for 5-6 minutes on each side until the internal temperature reaches 165°F (74°C) and the meat is golden brown. Remove from the skillet and let it rest.

Make the Sage Brown Butter:

- In the same skillet, add the remaining butter. Allow it to melt and start to brown slightly, about 2-3 minutes.
- Add the sage leaves and cook until crispy, releasing their aroma into the butter.

Serve:

- Slice the rested pheasant breast and drizzle with sage brown butter.
- Garnish with lemon zest if desired, and serve immediately.

Scientific Note:

Pheasant is a lean game meat, providing a high-quality protein source with fewer calories and fat compared to other meats. It is rich in B vitamins, particularly niacin and B6, which are important for energy production and brain health.

Butter from grass-fed sources offers healthy fats that are essential for maintaining ketosis. The process of browning the butter enhances its flavor by creating nutty, aromatic compounds.

Sage contains antioxidants and has been used traditionally to support digestion and reduce inflammation. It adds depth of flavor to the dish while complementing the richness of the brown butter.

Nutritional Information (per serving):

- Calories: ~540
- Protein: 42g
- Total Fat: 40g
- Saturated Fat: 18g
- Carbohydrates: <1g
- Fiber: 0g

Wild Boar Tenderloin with Dijon Mustard Sauce

Serves: 1

Cooking Time: 35 minutes

Ingredients and Portions/Measurements:

- **Wild Boar Tenderloin:** 6 oz (Rich in lean protein and iron, with a distinctive flavor)
- **Ghee:** 2 tablespoons (Provides healthy fats and enhances flavor)
- **Salt (Himalayan or Sea Salt):** 1/4 teaspoon (Contains essential trace minerals)
- **Black Pepper: To** taste (Enhances flavor)
- **Dijon Mustard:** 1 tablespoon (Adds tanginess and depth of flavor)
- **Heavy Cream:** 1/4 cup (Adds richness and healthy fats)
- **White Wine Vinegar:** 1 teaspoon (Adds acidity to balance flavors)

- **Fresh Tarragon:** 1 teaspoon, chopped (Optional garnish for added flavor)

Instructions:

Prepare the Wild Boar:

- Season the wild boar tenderloin with salt and pepper on all sides.
- Preheat a skillet over medium-high heat.

Cook the Wild Boar:

- Add the ghee to the skillet and allow it to melt.
- Add the wild boar tenderloin and sear for 4-5 minutes on each side until golden brown and the internal temperature reaches 145°F (63°C) for medium-rare.
- Remove the tenderloin from the skillet and let it rest.

Make the Dijon Mustard Sauce:

- In the same skillet, reduce the heat to low. Add the Dijon mustard, heavy cream, and white wine vinegar.
- Stir continuously, scraping up any browned bits from the bottom of the pan, and cook until the sauce is slightly thickened, about 3-4 minutes.

Serve:

- Slice the wild boar tenderloin and arrange it on a plate.
- Drizzle with the Dijon mustard sauce and garnish with fresh tarragon if desired. Serve immediately.

Scientific Note:

Wild Boar is a game meat that is leaner than conventional pork, providing a rich source of protein and essential nutrients like iron, which is crucial for oxygen transport and energy production.

Dijon Mustard offers a tangy flavor without adding carbohydrates, making it an ideal ingredient for maintaining ketosis. It also contains trace amounts of selenium, which supports thyroid function.

Heavy Cream adds a creamy texture and healthy fats that are essential for a Ketovore diet. It helps to maintain energy levels and supports the absorption of fat-soluble vitamins.

Nutritional Information (per serving):

- Calories: ~580
- Protein: 48g
- Total Fat: 42g
- Saturated Fat: 20g
- Carbohydrates: 2g
- Fiber: 0g

Kangaroo Steak with Bacon-Wrapped Asparagus

Serves: 1

Cooking Time: 30 minutes

Ingredients and Portions/Measurements:

- **Kangaroo Steak:** 6 oz (Lean protein source, rich in iron and omega-3 fatty acids)
- **Bacon Slices:** 2 (Provides healthy fats and enhances flavor)
- **Asparagus Spears:** 4 (Low in carbohydrates, provides vitamins and minerals)
- **Ghee:** 1 tablespoon (Adds healthy fats and a rich flavor)
- **Salt (Himalayan or Sea Salt):** 1/4 teaspoon (Contains essential trace minerals)
- **Black Pepper:** To taste (Enhances flavor)
- **Lemon Zest:** 1/2 teaspoon (Optional garnish for freshness)

Instructions:

Prepare the Asparagus:

- Preheat your oven to 400°F (200°C).
- Wrap each asparagus spear with a slice of bacon. Place them on a baking sheet.

Cook the Bacon-Wrapped Asparagus:

- Bake in the preheated oven for 10-12 minutes, or until the bacon is crispy and the asparagus is tender.

Prepare the Kangaroo Steak:

- Season the kangaroo steak with salt and pepper on both sides.
- Heat a skillet over medium-high heat and add the ghee.

Cook the Kangaroo Steak:

- Add the kangaroo steak to the hot skillet and cook for 3-4 minutes on each side for medium-rare, or adjust the time based on your preferred level of doneness.
- Remove from the skillet and let it rest for a few minutes.

Serve:

- Slice the kangaroo steak and arrange it on a plate with the bacon-wrapped asparagus.

- Garnish with lemon zest if desired, and serve immediately.

Scientific Note:

Kangaroo Steak is a lean game meat that is high in protein and low in fat, making it a nutrient-dense option for those on a Ketovore diet. It provides omega-3 fatty acids, which support heart health and reduce inflammation.

Bacon adds flavor and healthy fats, essential for maintaining ketosis and providing energy. It complements the lean kangaroo meat, creating a balanced meal.

Asparagus is a low-carbohydrate vegetable rich in vitamins A, C, and K, as well as fiber and antioxidants, supporting overall health and digestion.

Nutritional Information (per serving):

- Calories: ~520
- Protein: 48g
- Total Fat: 38g
- Saturated Fat: 16g
- Carbohydrates: 3g
- Fiber: 1g

Pork Belly with Spiced Lamb Sausage

Serves: 1

Cooking Time: 40 minutes

Ingredients and Portions/Measurements:

- **Pork Belly:** 6 oz (Rich in healthy fats and protein, provides energy and flavor)
- **Lamb Sausage:** 4 oz (High-quality protein source, rich in iron and B vitamins)
- **Olive Oil: 1** tablespoon (Adds healthy fats and enhances flavor)
- **Salt (Himalayan or Sea Salt):** 1/4 teaspoon (Contains essential trace minerals)
- **Black Pepper:** To taste (Enhances flavor)
- **Cumin:** 1/2 teaspoon (Adds warmth and supports digestion)
- **Paprika:** 1/4 teaspoon (Adds smokiness and depth of flavor)

- **Fresh Mint:** 1 tablespoon, chopped (Optional garnish for freshness and nutrients)

Instructions:

Prepare the Pork Belly:

- Preheat your oven to 375°F (190°C).
- Score the skin of the pork belly in a crosshatch pattern without cutting into the meat. Season with salt, pepper, and cumin.

Cook the Pork Belly:

- Heat olive oil in an oven-safe skillet over medium-high heat.
- Place the pork belly skin-side down and sear until golden brown and crispy, about 5-7 minutes.
- Transfer the skillet to the oven and roast for 20-25 minutes, or until the pork belly is tender and cooked through.

Cook the Lamb Sausage:

- In a separate skillet over medium heat, add the lamb sausage and cook until browned and cooked through, about 8-10 minutes.
- Sprinkle with paprika while cooking for added flavor.

Serve:

- Slice the roasted pork belly and place it on a plate with the spiced lamb sausage.
- Garnish with fresh mint if desired, and serve immediately.

Scientific Note:

Pork Belly is a flavorful cut of meat that provides healthy fats and energy for those on a Ketovore diet. The fat content helps maintain ketosis and provides essential fatty acids for overall health.

Lamb Sausage offers a unique source of protein and is rich in essential nutrients like iron and B vitamins. The spices used in this recipe add depth of flavor and support digestion.

Cumin and Paprika are spices that enhance the flavor profile of the dish while offering antioxidant properties and aiding in digestion.

Nutritional Information (per serving):

- Calories: ~780
- Protein: 50g
- Total Fat: 65g
- Saturated Fat: 25g
- Carbohydrates: 1g
- Fiber: 0g

Veal Sweetbreads with Herb-Infused Ghee

Serves: 1

Cooking Time: 45 minutes

Ingredients and Portions/Measurements:

- **Veal Sweetbreads:** 6 oz (Rich in high-quality protein, B vitamins, and selenium)
- **Ghee:** 2 tablespoons (Provides healthy fats and a rich, buttery flavor)
- **Salt (Himalayan or Sea Salt):** 1/4 teaspoon (Contains essential trace minerals)
- **Black Pepper:** To taste (Enhances flavor)
- **Fresh Thyme:** 1 tablespoon, chopped (For flavor and antioxidants)
- **Fresh Sage:** 5-6 leaves (Adds earthy flavor and aids digestion)
- **Lemon Wedges:** For serving (Optional for a fresh contrast)

Instructions:

Prepare the Sweetbreads:

- Soak the sweetbreads in cold water for 30 minutes, changing the water once to remove impurities.
- Bring a pot of water to a gentle simmer and poach the sweetbreads for 5 minutes. Remove from water and cool slightly.

Cook the Sweetbreads:

- Pat the sweetbreads dry with paper towels and season with salt and pepper.
- Heat ghee in a skillet over medium heat. Add the thyme and sage, allowing the herbs to infuse the ghee for 1-2 minutes.
- Add the sweetbreads to the skillet and cook for 4-5 minutes on each side until golden brown and crispy.

Serve:

- Plate the sweetbreads and drizzle with herb-infused ghee from the skillet.
- Serve with lemon wedges for a fresh, zesty contrast, if desired.

Scientific Note:

Veal Sweetbreads are a delicacy rich in high-quality protein, essential for muscle maintenance and repair. They also provide important micronutrients like selenium, which supports immune function and antioxidant defense.

Ghee is a source of healthy fats that aid in maintaining ketosis. The infusion of herbs like thyme and sage not only adds flavor but also provides antioxidants and aids in digestion.

Fresh Herbs like thyme and sage contain bioactive compounds that can support digestion and reduce inflammation, making them beneficial additions to a Ketovore diet.

Nutritional Information (per serving):

- Calories: ~520
- Protein: 40g
- Total Fat: 40g
- Saturated Fat: 20g
- Carbohydrates: 1g
- Fiber: 0g

Bison Burger with Egg and Hollandaise Sauce

Serves: 1

Cooking Time: 30 minutes

Ingredients and Portions/Measurements:

- **Ground Bison**: 6 oz (Lean protein source, rich in iron and B vitamins)
- **Egg**: 1 large (Provides high-quality protein and healthy fats)
- **Butter (Grass-fed)**: 3 tablespoons (Adds healthy fats and a rich, buttery flavor)
- **Lemon Juice**: 1 tablespoon (Adds acidity to balance flavors)
- **Salt (Himalayan or Sea Salt)**: 1/4 teaspoon (Contains essential trace minerals)
- **Black Pepper**: To taste (Enhances flavor)
- **Smoked Paprika**: 1/4 teaspoon (Adds smokiness and depth of flavor)
- **Fresh Chives**: 1 tablespoon, chopped (Optional garnish for freshness)

Instructions:

Prepare the Bison Burger:

- Season the ground bison with salt, pepper, and smoked paprika. Form into a patty.
- Heat a skillet over medium-high heat and cook the bison patty for 4-5 minutes on each side until cooked to your desired level of doneness.

Poach the Egg:

- Bring a small pot of water to a gentle simmer. Add a splash of vinegar (optional) to help the egg hold its shape.
- Crack the egg into a small bowl and gently slide it into the simmering water. Cook for 3-4 minutes until the white is set but the yolk is still runny. Remove with a slotted spoon and set aside.

Make the Hollandaise Sauce:

- Melt the butter in a saucepan over low heat. In a small bowl, whisk together the lemon juice, a pinch of salt, and a little black pepper.
- Slowly drizzle the melted butter into the lemon mixture, whisking continuously until the sauce is smooth and creamy.

Assemble the Dish:

- Place the cooked bison patty on a plate and top with the poached egg.
- Drizzle the hollandaise sauce over the top and garnish with chopped chives if desired.

Scientific Note:

Bison is a lean source of protein that provides essential nutrients such as iron and B vitamins, which support energy metabolism and overall health. It is lower in fat and calories than traditional beef, making it a great option for a Ketovore diet.

Eggs offer high-quality protein and healthy fats, promoting satiety and providing a steady source of energy. The yolk is also rich in vitamins and minerals, including choline, which supports brain health.

Hollandaise Sauce made with butter adds healthy fats essential for maintaining ketosis. The acidity from the lemon juice balances the richness of the dish, while providing vitamin C.

Nutritional Information (per serving):

- Calories: ~650
- Protein: 45g
- Total Fat: 50g
- Saturated Fat: 22g
- Carbohydrates: <1g
- Fiber: 0g

CHAPTER 4

SNACKS AND DIPS

Crispy Chicken Skin Chips with Beef Tallow Aioli

Serves: 1

Cooking Time: 25 minutes

Ingredients and Portions/Measurements:

- **Chicken Skin**: 4 oz (High in healthy fats and collagen)
- **Beef Tallow**: 1/4 cup (Provides healthy saturated fats and adds a rich flavor)
- **Egg Yolk**: 1 large (Emulsifies the aioli, providing protein and fats)
- **Lemon Juice**: 1 teaspoon (Adds acidity and brightness)
- **Salt (Himalayan or Sea Salt)**: 1/4 teaspoon (Contains essential trace minerals)

- **Garlic Powder**: 1/4 teaspoon (Adds flavor without carbs)
- **Fresh Chives**: 1 tablespoon, chopped (Optional garnish for freshness and flavor)

Instructions:

Prepare the Chicken Skin Chips:

- Preheat the oven to 375°F (190°C).
- Place the chicken skin on a baking sheet lined with parchment paper. Sprinkle with salt and garlic powder.
- Bake for 15-20 minutes or until crispy and golden brown. Remove from the oven and let cool.

Make the Beef Tallow Aioli:

- In a small bowl, whisk together the egg yolk and lemon juice until smooth.
- Slowly drizzle in the melted beef tallow while whisking continuously until the mixture emulsifies and thickens. Season with salt.

Serve:

- Serve the crispy chicken skin chips with a side of beef tallow aioli for dipping.
- Garnish with chopped chives if desired.

Scientific Note:

Chicken Skin is a great source of collagen and healthy fats, providing nutrients that support skin health and joint function. The fats in chicken skin are predominantly monounsaturated and saturated fats, which are beneficial for maintaining ketosis.

Beef Tallow is rich in saturated fats and provides a stable fat source that is excellent for cooking and making sauces. It supports the absorption of fat-soluble vitamins and contributes to satiety.

Egg Yolk in the aioli provides lecithin, which helps emulsify the sauce and adds essential vitamins and minerals, including vitamin D and choline, which support brain health.

Nutritional Information (per serving):

- Calories: ~450
- Protein: 12g
- Total Fat: 42g
- Saturated Fat: 20g
- Carbohydrates: 1g
- Fiber: 0g

Venison Jerky Bites with Liver Pâté

Serves: 1

Cooking Time: 45 minutes (plus marinating time)

Ingredients and Portions/Measurements:

- **Venison Strips:** 4 oz (High in lean protein and essential nutrients)
- **Liver (Chicken or Beef):** 2 oz (Rich in vitamins A, B12, and iron)
- **Ghee:** 1 tablespoon (Provides healthy fats and enhances flavor)
- **Apple Cider Vinegar:** 1 tablespoon (Adds acidity and tenderizes meat)
- **Salt (Himalayan or Sea Salt):** 1/4 teaspoon (Contains essential trace minerals)
- **Black Pepper:** To taste (Enhances flavor)

- **Dried Thyme**: 1/2 teaspoon (Adds earthy flavor and antioxidants)
- **Garlic Powder**: 1/4 teaspoon (Adds flavor without carbs)
- **Fresh Parsley**: 1 tablespoon, chopped (Optional garnish for freshness)

Instructions:

Marinate the Venison:

- In a bowl, combine apple cider vinegar, salt, black pepper, dried thyme, and garlic powder.
- Add venison strips to the marinade and let them sit for at least 1 hour in the refrigerator.

Prepare the Venison Jerky:

- Preheat your oven to 175°F (80°C).
- Lay the marinated venison strips on a baking rack placed over a baking sheet.
- Bake for 2-3 hours or until the venison is dry and chewy.

Make the Liver Pâté:

- In a skillet, melt ghee over medium heat. Add liver pieces and cook until browned and cooked through.
- Transfer cooked liver to a food processor. Blend until smooth, adding salt and pepper to taste.

Serve:

- Serve venison jerky bites with a side of liver pâté for dipping.
- Garnish with fresh parsley if desired, and enjoy!

Scientific Note:

Venison is a lean source of protein that provides essential nutrients like zinc and iron, which support immune function and energy metabolism. Its low fat content makes it ideal for maintaining a high-protein, low-carb diet.

Liver is one of the most nutrient-dense foods available, rich in vitamins A and B12, which are crucial for vision, skin health, and energy production. It also provides iron, which is essential for oxygen transport in the body.

Ghee offers healthy saturated fats that help maintain ketosis and provide a steady source of energy. It also supports the absorption of fat-soluble vitamins found in liver.

Nutritional Information (per serving):

- Calories: ~350
- Protein: 35g
- Total Fat: 20g
- Saturated Fat: 10g
- Carbohydrates: <1g
- Fiber: 0g

Pork Rind Nachos with Duck Fat Guacamole

Serves: 1

Cooking Time: 20 minutes

Ingredients and Portions/Measurements:

- **Pork Rinds:** 2 oz (Crispy and high in protein, low in carbohydrates)
- **Duck Fat:** 1 tablespoon (Adds rich flavor and healthy fats)
- **Avocado:** 1/2, mashed (Rich in healthy fats and fiber)
- **Lime Juice:** 1 teaspoon (Adds acidity and freshness)
- **Salt (Himalayan or Sea Salt):** 1/4 teaspoon (Contains essential trace minerals)
- **Smoked Paprika:** 1/4 teaspoon (Adds smokiness and depth of flavor)
- **Fresh Cilantro:** 1 tablespoon, chopped (Optional garnish for flavor and nutrients)
- **Jalapeño:** 1 small, finely chopped (Adds spice, optional)

Instructions:

Prepare the Duck Fat Guacamole:

- In a bowl, mash the avocado and mix it with lime juice, duck fat, salt, smoked paprika, and jalapeño (if using) until smooth.

Assemble the Pork Rind Nachos:

- Spread the pork rinds on a serving plate.

Serve:

- Dollop the duck fat guacamole over the pork rinds and garnish with fresh cilantro if desired.
- Serve immediately and enjoy the crunchy, creamy combination.

Scientific Note:

Pork Rinds are a great snack option for a Ketovore diet as they are high in protein and contain no carbohydrates. They are made by frying or roasting pork skin, resulting in a crunchy texture and savory flavor.

Duck Fat is a healthy source of monounsaturated fats, similar to olive oil, and adds a rich flavor to dishes. It supports heart health and provides energy.

Avocado is rich in monounsaturated fats and provides fiber, making it an excellent addition to a Ketovore diet.

It also contains potassium, which helps maintain electrolyte balance.

Nutritional Information (per serving):

- Calories: ~400
- Protein: 20g
- Total Fat: 36g
- Saturated Fat: 12g
- Carbohydrates: 3g
- Fiber: 2g

Seared Beef Heart Skewers with Bone Marrow Dip

Serves: 1

Cooking Time: 30 minutes

Ingredients and Portions/Measurements:

- **Beef Heart**: 4 oz, cubed (Rich in lean protein and essential nutrients)
- **Bone Marrow**: 2 tablespoons (Provides healthy fats and a rich flavor)
- **Olive Oil**: 1 tablespoon (Adds healthy fats and enhances flavor)
- **Salt (Himalayan or Sea Salt)**: 1/4 teaspoon (Contains essential trace minerals)
- **Black Pepper**: To taste (Enhances flavor)
- **Rosemary**: 1/2 teaspoon, chopped (Adds an earthy flavor and antioxidants)
- **Garlic Powder**: 1/4 teaspoon (Adds flavor without carbs)
- **Lemon Juice**: 1 teaspoon (Optional for a fresh, zesty contrast)

Instructions:

Prepare the Beef Heart Skewers:

- Season the beef heart cubes with olive oil, salt, black pepper, rosemary, and garlic powder.
- Thread the seasoned beef heart onto skewers.

Sear the Beef Heart:

- Preheat a skillet or grill over medium-high heat.
- Sear the beef heart skewers for 3-4 minutes on each side until browned and cooked to your preferred level of doneness. Remove from heat and set aside.

Make the Bone Marrow Dip:

- In a small saucepan, melt the bone marrow over low heat until it becomes liquid.

- Season with a pinch of salt and lemon juice for added brightness.

Serve:

- Serve the seared beef heart skewers with the bone marrow dip on the side.

- Enjoy immediately for a rich and savory snack experience.

Scientific Note:

Beef Heart is a highly nutritious organ meat that is rich in protein and essential nutrients like iron, zinc, and CoQ10, which support heart health and energy metabolism. Its lean composition makes it suitable for a Ketovore diet.

Bone Marrow is a nutrient-dense source of healthy fats and collagen, which supports joint health and provides energy. It is rich in fat-soluble vitamins and contributes to the rich flavor of the dip.

Rosemary is an herb with antioxidant properties that can aid digestion and reduce inflammation, making it a flavorful and beneficial addition to the dish.

Nutritional Information (per serving):

- Calories: ~480

- Protein: 32g

- Total Fat: 38g

- Saturated Fat: 15g

- Carbohydrates: <1g

- Fiber: 0g

Crispy Chicken Livers with Lemon Herb Dip

Serves: 1

Cooking Time: 25 minutes

Ingredients and Portions/Measurements:

- **Chicken Livers:** 4 oz (Rich in vitamins A, B12, and iron)

- **Lard:** 2 tablespoons (Provides healthy fats for cooking)

- **Salt (Himalayan or Sea Salt):** 1/4 teaspoon (Contains essential trace minerals)

- **Black Pepper:** To taste (Enhances flavor)

- **Lemon Juice:** 1 tablespoon (Adds acidity and freshness)

- **Mayonnaise (Homemade or Ketovore-friendly):** 2 tablespoons (Adds creaminess and healthy fats)

- **Fresh Dill:** 1 teaspoon, chopped (Adds flavor and nutrients)
- **Garlic Powder:** 1/4 teaspoon (Adds flavor without carbs)

Instructions:

Prepare the Chicken Livers:

- Rinse the chicken livers under cold water and pat dry with paper towels.
- Season with salt and black pepper.

Cook the Chicken Livers:

- Heat lard in a skillet over medium-high heat.
- Add chicken livers and cook for 4-5 minutes on each side until crispy and cooked through. Remove from the skillet and let cool slightly.

Make the Lemon Herb Dip:

- In a small bowl, combine mayonnaise, lemon juice, fresh dill, and garlic powder.
- Mix until smooth and well combined.

Serve:

- Serve the crispy chicken livers with lemon herb dip on the side.
- Enjoy immediately for a flavorful and nutritious snack.

Scientific Note:

Chicken Livers are a nutrient powerhouse, offering high levels of vitamins A and B12, which are essential for vision, immune function, and energy metabolism. They are also an excellent source of iron, crucial for oxygen transport in the body.

Lard is a traditional cooking fat rich in monounsaturated and saturated fats, supporting energy levels and maintaining ketosis. It provides a stable fat source for high-heat cooking.

Mayonnaise provides healthy fats and creaminess to the dip, making it a perfect accompaniment to the crispy livers. It is important to choose a mayonnaise that aligns with Ketovore principles, such as homemade or one made with animal-based fats.

Nutritional Information (per serving):

- Calories: ~400
- Protein: 28g
- Total Fat: 32g
- Saturated Fat: 10g
- Carbohydrates: <1g
- Fiber: 0g

Smoked Duck Breast Bites with Creamy Bacon Dip

Serves: 1

Cooking Time: 20 minutes

Ingredients and Portions/Measurements:

- **Smoked Duck Breast**: 4 oz, thinly sliced (Rich in protein and healthy fats)
- **Bacon**: 2 slices (Adds flavor and fat)
- **Cream Cheese**: 2 tablespoons (Provides creaminess and fats)
- **Heavy Cream**: 1 tablespoon (Adds richness)
- **Salt (Himalayan or Sea Salt)**: 1/4 teaspoon (Contains essential trace minerals)
- **Black Pepper**: To taste (Enhances flavor)
- **Chives**: 1 tablespoon, chopped (Optional garnish for freshness)

Instructions:

Prepare the Smoked Duck Breast:

- Slice the smoked duck breast into bite-sized pieces and set aside.

Cook the Bacon:

- In a skillet over medium heat, cook the bacon until crispy. Remove from the skillet and crumble into small pieces.

Make the Creamy Bacon Dip:

- In a small saucepan, heat the cream cheese and heavy cream over low heat, stirring until smooth.
- Stir in the crumbled bacon, salt, and black pepper.

Serve:

- Arrange the smoked duck breast bites on a plate.
- Serve with the creamy bacon dip on the side, garnished with chopped chives if desired.

Scientific Note:

Smoked Duck Breast is a nutrient-dense source of protein and healthy fats, providing essential fatty acids and micronutrients that support metabolic health and satiety.

Bacon adds a savory depth to the dip while contributing additional healthy fats, which are important for maintaining ketosis.

Cream Cheese and Heavy Cream offer rich sources of fat and protein, helping to create a satisfying, creamy dip that complements the smoky flavor of the duck.

Nutritional Information (per serving):

- Calories: ~550
- Protein: 32g
- Total Fat: 45g
- Saturated Fat: 20g
- Carbohydrates: 2g
- Fiber: 0g

Grilled Octopus Skewers with Caper Herb Dip

Serves: 1

Cooking Time: 35 minutes

Ingredients and Portions/Measurements:

- **Octopus Tentacles:** 4 oz (Rich in lean protein and essential minerals)
- **Olive Oil:** 2 tablespoons (Adds healthy fats and enhances flavor)
- **Salt (Himalayan or Sea Salt):** 1/4 teaspoon (Contains essential trace minerals)
- **Black Pepper:** To taste (Enhances flavor)
- **Fresh Lemon Juice:** 1 tablespoon (Adds acidity and brightness)
- **Capers:** 1 tablespoon (Adds tanginess and flavor)
- **Parsley:** 2 tablespoons, chopped (Adds flavor and nutrients)
- **Garlic Clove:** 1, minced (Adds flavor and beneficial compounds)

Instructions:

Prepare the Octopus:

- Bring a pot of water to a boil. Add the octopus tentacles and cook for 10-15 minutes until tender.
- Drain and pat the octopus dry with paper towels.

Grill the Octopus:

- Preheat a grill or grill pan over medium-high heat.
- Toss the octopus with olive oil, salt, and black pepper.
- Grill the octopus for 3-4 minutes on each side until charred and cooked through.

Make the Caper Herb Dip:

- In a small bowl, combine minced garlic, chopped parsley, capers, lemon juice, and 1 tablespoon of olive oil.
- Mix well and season with salt and pepper to taste.

Serve:

- Arrange the grilled octopus skewers on a plate.
- Serve with the caper herb dip on the side for dipping.

Scientific Note:

Octopus is a lean source of protein, rich in essential minerals like selenium, which supports immune function and acts as an antioxidant. It is also a good source of B vitamins, important for energy metabolism.

Capers add a tangy flavor to the dip and are low in calories, providing a burst of flavor without adding carbohydrates.

Olive Oil is rich in monounsaturated fats, which support heart health and provide a steady source of energy in a Ketovore diet.

Nutritional Information (per serving):

- Calories: ~400
- Protein: 30g
- Total Fat: 30g
- Saturated Fat: 4g
- Carbohydrates: 3g

- Fiber: 1g

Chicharrón with Bone Broth Cheese Dip

Serves: 1

Cooking Time: 15 minutes

Ingredients and Portions/Measurements:

- Chicharrón (Pork Rinds): 2 oz (Crunchy, low-carb snack rich in protein)
- Bone Broth: 1/4 cup (Rich in collagen and minerals)
- Cream Cheese: 2 tablespoons (Adds creaminess and healthy fats)
- Gruyère Cheese: 1/4 cup, shredded (Adds rich flavor and healthy fats)
- Salt (Himalayan or Sea Salt): 1/4 teaspoon (Contains essential trace minerals)
- Black Pepper: To taste (Enhances flavor)
- Nutmeg: A pinch (Adds warmth and depth of flavor)

Instructions:

Prepare the Bone Broth Cheese Dip:

- In a small saucepan, heat the bone broth over medium heat until warm.
- Add the cream cheese and Gruyère cheese, stirring continuously until the cheese is melted and the mixture is smooth.
- Season with salt, black pepper, and a pinch of nutmeg.

Serve:

- Pour the warm cheese dip into a small bowl.
- Serve the chicharrón alongside the dip for a crunchy, savory snack.

Scientific Note:

Chicharrón (Pork Rinds) are a great low-carb snack option for a Ketovore diet as they are high in protein and fat, providing a crunchy texture and savory flavor without carbohydrates.

Bone Broth is rich in collagen and minerals such as calcium and magnesium, which support joint health and overall wellness. It adds depth of flavor and nutrition to the cheese dip.

Gruyère Cheese is a good source of calcium and healthy fats, making it an excellent addition to a Ketovore diet. It provides a creamy texture and rich flavor to the dip.

Nutritional Information (per serving):

- Calories: ~480
- Protein: 30g
- Total Fat: 40g
- Saturated Fat: 18g
- Carbohydrates: 2g
- Fiber: 0g

Lamb Meatballs with Creamy Tallow Dip

Serves: 1

Cooking Time: 30 minutes

Ingredients and Portions/Measurements:

- **Ground Lamb:** 4 oz (Rich in protein and healthy fats)
- **Beef Tallow:** 2 tablespoons (Provides healthy fats and adds a rich flavor)
- **Egg Yolk:** 1 large (Adds richness and binds the meatballs)

- **Salt (Himalayan or Sea Salt):** 1/4 teaspoon (Contains essential trace minerals)
- **Black Pepper:** To taste (Enhances flavor)
- Cumin: 1/2 teaspoon (Adds warmth and depth)
- **Fresh Mint:** 1 tablespoon, chopped (Optional for garnish)
- **Lemon Zest:** 1/2 teaspoon (Optional for freshness)

Instructions:

Prepare the Lamb Meatballs:

- In a bowl, combine ground lamb, egg yolk, salt, black pepper, and cumin.
- Mix well and form into small meatballs.

Cook the Meatballs:

- Heat 1 tablespoon of beef tallow in a skillet over medium heat.
- Add the meatballs and cook for 8-10 minutes, turning occasionally, until browned and cooked through. Remove from the skillet and set aside.

Make the Creamy Tallow Dip:

- In the same skillet, add the remaining beef tallow and melt over low heat.
- Pour the melted tallow into a small bowl and let it cool slightly.

Serve:

- Serve the lamb meatballs with the creamy tallow dip on the side.
- Garnish with fresh mint and lemon zest if desired.

Scientific Note:

Lamb is an excellent source of high-quality protein and provides essential nutrients such as iron, zinc, and B vitamins, which support energy production and immune function.

Beef Tallow is a nutrient-dense fat rich in conjugated linoleic acid (CLA) and omega-3 fatty acids, which have anti-inflammatory properties and support heart health.

Egg Yolk provides lecithin, which acts as an emulsifier, adding richness and helping to bind the meatballs. It is also rich in vitamins and minerals, including choline, which supports brain health.

Nutritional Information (per serving):

- Calories: ~500
- Protein: 35g
- Total Fat: 40g
- Saturated Fat: 18g
- Carbohydrates: 1g
- Fiber: 0g

Baked Salmon Skin Chips with Dill Cream Dip

Serves: 1

Cooking Time: 25 minutes

Ingredients and Portions/Measurements:

- **Salmon Skin:** From 1 fillet (Rich in omega-3 fatty acids)
- **Olive Oil:** 1 tablespoon (Provides healthy fats and enhances crispiness)
- **Salt (Himalayan or Sea Salt):** 1/4 teaspoon (Contains essential trace minerals)
- **Black Pepper:** To taste (Enhances flavor)

Dill Cream Dip:

- **Sour Cream:** 2 tablespoons (Adds creaminess and healthy fats)
- **Fresh Dill:** 1 tablespoon, chopped (Provides freshness and flavor)
- **Lemon Juice:** 1 teaspoon (Adds acidity and brightness)
- **Garlic Powder:** 1/4 teaspoon (Adds flavor without carbs)

Instructions:

Prepare the Salmon Skin Chips:

- Preheat your oven to 375°F (190°C).
- Pat the salmon skin dry with paper towels. Brush both sides with olive oil and season with salt and black pepper.
- Place the salmon skin on a baking sheet lined with parchment paper, skin-side up.

Bake the Salmon Skin:

- Bake in the preheated oven for 10-15 minutes until the skin is crispy and golden brown. Remove from the oven and let it cool slightly.

Prepare the Dill Cream Dip:

- In a small bowl, combine sour cream, fresh dill, lemon juice, and garlic powder.
- Mix until smooth and well combined.

Serve:

- Break the crispy salmon skin into bite-sized pieces.
- Serve with the dill cream dip on the side for a refreshing contrast.

Scientific Note:

Salmon Skin is a rich source of omega-3 fatty acids, which have anti-inflammatory properties and support heart and brain health. It provides a crispy texture and savory flavor when baked.

Olive Oil is high in monounsaturated fats, promoting heart health and providing a stable fat source for high-heat cooking.

Sour Cream adds creaminess to the dip and provides healthy fats that support ketosis. It pairs well with fresh dill and lemon juice, offering a refreshing contrast to the savory salmon skin.

Nutritional Information (per serving):

- Calories: ~420
- Protein: 15g
- Total Fat: 38g
- Saturated Fat: 10g
- Cholesterol: 50mg
- Carbohydrates: 2g
- Fiber: 0g
- Sodium: 350mg

CHAPTER 5

DINNER RECIPES

Herb-Crusted Rack of Elk with Garlic Butter Sauce

Serves: 1

Cooking Time: 45 minutes

Ingredients and Portions/Measurements:

- **Rack of Elk**: 8 oz (Lean protein source, rich in iron and omega-3 fatty acids)
- **Butter (Grass-fed)**: 3 tablespoons (Adds healthy fats and richness)
- **Salt (Himalayan or Sea Salt)**: 1/4 teaspoon (Contains essential trace minerals)
- **Black Pepper**: To taste (Enhances flavor)
- **Fresh Rosemary**: 1 tablespoon, chopped (Adds aroma and antioxidants)

- Fresh Thyme: 1 tablespoon, chopped (Enhances flavor and adds nutrients)
- Garlic Cloves: 2, minced (Adds flavor and beneficial compounds)
- Lemon Zest: 1/2 teaspoon (Optional for freshness and brightness)

Instructions:

Prepare the Elk:

- Preheat the oven to 400°F (200°C).
- Season the rack of elk with salt, black pepper, rosemary, and thyme, pressing the herbs onto the meat to form a crust.

Sear the Elk:

- Heat 1 tablespoon of butter in an oven-safe skillet over medium-high heat.
- Add the elk and sear for 2-3 minutes on each side until browned.

Roast the Elk:

- Transfer the skillet to the preheated oven and roast for 15-20 minutes, or until the internal temperature reaches 135°F (57°C) for medium-rare.
- Remove the elk from the oven and let it rest for 5 minutes before slicing.

Make the Garlic Butter Sauce:

- In a small saucepan, melt the remaining 2 tablespoons of butter over low heat.

- Add minced garlic and cook until fragrant, about 1 minute. Remove from heat.

Serve:

- Slice the elk and arrange it on a plate.
- Drizzle with garlic butter sauce and garnish with lemon zest if desired.

Scientific Note

Elk is a lean and nutrient-dense game meat that provides high-quality protein and essential nutrients like iron, which supports oxygen transport and energy production. Its low fat content and high omega-3 fatty acid profile make it an excellent choice for a Ketovore diet.

Butter from grass-fed sources is rich in conjugated linoleic acid (CLA) and omega-3 fatty acids, both of which have anti-inflammatory properties and support heart health.

Herbs like rosemary and thyme add flavor and antioxidants, which can help reduce inflammation and support overall health.

Nutritional Information (per serving):

- Calories: ~650
- Protein: 55g
- Total Fat: 48g
- Saturated Fat: 22g
- Carbohydrates: <1g
- Fiber: 0g

Pan-Seared Swordfish with Anchovy Herb Butter

Serves: 1

Cooking Time: 30 minutes

Ingredients and Portions/Measurements:

- **Swordfish Steak:** 8 oz (Rich in lean protein and omega-3 fatty acids)
- **Anchovy Fillets:** 2 (Provides umami flavor and essential fatty acids)
- **Butter (Grass-fed):** 2 tablespoons (Adds healthy fats and rich flavor)
- **Salt (Himalayan or Sea Salt):** 1/4 teaspoon (Contains essential trace minerals)
- **Black Pepper:** To taste (Enhances flavor)
- **Fresh Basil:** 1 tablespoon, chopped (Adds aroma and antioxidants)
- **Lemon Juice:** 1 tablespoon (Adds acidity and brightness)
- **Olive Oil:** 1 tablespoon (Provides healthy fats and aids cooking)

Instructions:

- Prepare the Swordfish:
- Season the swordfish steak with salt and black pepper on both sides.
- Heat olive oil in a skillet over medium-high heat.

Cook the Swordfish:

- Add the swordfish steak to the hot skillet and sear for 4-5 minutes on each side, until golden brown and cooked through. Remove from the skillet and set aside.

Make the Anchovy Herb Butter:

- In the same skillet, melt the butter over low heat.
- Add anchovy fillets and mash them with a fork until dissolved.
- Stir in fresh basil and lemon juice, mixing well.

Serve

- Place the swordfish on a plate and drizzle with the anchovy herb butter.
- Serve immediately for a flavorful and nutritious dinner.

Scientific Note:

Swordfish is a nutrient-rich fish providing high-quality protein and essential omega-3 fatty acids, which support cardiovascular health and reduce inflammation. It is also a good source of selenium, an antioxidant that helps protect cells from damage.

Anchovies are rich in omega-3 fatty acids and add a savory, umami flavor to dishes. They contribute to heart health by reducing triglycerides and supporting brain function.

Butter from grass-fed sources contains conjugated linoleic acid (CLA) and omega-3 fatty acids, both of which have anti-inflammatory properties and support overall health.

Nutritional Information (per serving):

- Calories: ~600
- Protein: 50g
- Total Fat: 44g
- Saturated Fat: 18g
- Carbohydrates: <1g
- Fiber: 0g

Wild Boar Chops with Mustard Cream Sauce

Serves: 1

Cooking Time: 35 minutes

Ingredients and Portions/Measurements:

- **Wild Boar Chops:** 8 oz (Rich in lean protein and iron)
- **Butter (Grass-fed):** 3 tablespoons (Provides healthy fats and flavor)
- **Salt (Himalayan or Sea Salt):** 1/4 teaspoon (Contains essential trace minerals)
- **Black Pepper:** To taste (Enhances flavor)
- **Dijon Mustard:** 1 tablespoon (Adds depth of flavor)
- **Heavy Cream:** 1/4 cup (Adds richness and healthy fats)
- **Fresh Thyme:** 1 teaspoon, chopped (Optional for garnish and flavor)

- **Garlic Clove:** 1, minced (Adds flavor and beneficial compounds)

Instructions:

- Prepare the Wild Boar Chops:
- Season the wild boar chops with salt and black pepper on both sides.
- Heat 1 tablespoon of butter in a skillet over medium-high heat.

Cook the Wild Boar Chops:

- Add the wild boar chops to the skillet and sear for 4-5 minutes on each side, until browned and cooked to your preferred level of doneness. Remove from the skillet and set aside.

Make the Mustard Cream Sauce:

- In the same skillet, melt the remaining butter over low heat.
- Add the minced garlic and cook until fragrant, about 1 minute.
- Stir in Dijon mustard and heavy cream, mixing well. Cook for 2-3 minutes until the sauce thickens slightly.

Serve:

- Place the wild boar chops on a plate and drizzle with the mustard cream sauce.
- Garnish with fresh thyme if desired and serve immediately.

Scientific Note:

Wild Boar is a nutrient-rich game meat that is lower in fat than conventional pork. It provides high-quality protein, iron, and B vitamins, supporting muscle maintenance and energy production.

Dijon Mustard offers a tangy flavor without adding carbohydrates, making it an ideal ingredient for maintaining ketosis. It contains antioxidants and trace minerals that support overall health.

Heavy Cream adds richness to the sauce and provides healthy fats that support energy and ketosis in a Ketovore diet.

Nutritional Information (per serving):

- Calories: ~700
- Protein: 50g
- Total Fat: 55g
- Saturated Fat: 25g
- Carbohydrates: 2g
- Fiber: 0g

Roasted Quail with Bacon-Wrapped Asparagus

Serves: 1

Cooking Time: 40 minutes

Ingredients and Portions/Measurements:

- Quail: 2 whole (Rich in lean protein and essential nutrients)
- Bacon: 4 slices (Provides healthy fats and flavor)
- Asparagus Spears: 8 (Low in carbohydrates, adds nutrients and fiber)
- Butter (Grass-fed): 2 tablespoons (Adds healthy fats and richness)
- Salt (Himalayan or Sea Salt): 1/4 teaspoon (Contains essential trace minerals)
- Black Pepper: To taste (Enhances flavor)
- Garlic Powder: 1/2 teaspoon (Adds flavor without carbs)
- Lemon Wedges: For serving (Optional for a fresh contrast)

Instructions:

Prepare the Quail:

- Preheat your oven to 375°F (190°C).
- Season the quail inside and out with salt, black pepper, and garlic powder.
- Rub the outside of each quail with butter.

Prepare the Asparagus:

- Wrap each asparagus spear with a slice of bacon.

Roast the Quail and Asparagus:

- Place the quail on a roasting pan and surround with the bacon-wrapped asparagus.
- Roast in the oven for 25-30 minutes, or until the quail is golden brown and cooked through, and the bacon is crispy.

Serve:

- Transfer the roasted quail and bacon-wrapped asparagus to a plate.
- Serve with lemon wedges for a fresh, zesty contrast.

Scientific Note:

Quail is a nutrient-dense poultry option, providing lean protein and essential nutrients like niacin and vitamin B6, which support energy metabolism and overall health.

Bacon adds savory flavor and healthy fats, which are important for maintaining ketosis and providing energy. It complements the lean quail, creating a balanced meal.

Asparagus is a low-carbohydrate vegetable rich in vitamins A, C, and K, as well as fiber and antioxidants, supporting overall health and digestion.

Nutritional Information (per serving):

- Calories: ~650
- Protein: 55g
- Total Fat: 48g
- Saturated Fat: 20g
- Carbohydrates: 4g
- Fiber: 2g

Grilled Venison Loin with Herb Butter

Serves: 1

Cooking Time: 30 minutes

Ingredients and Portions/Measurements:

- **Venison Loin:** 8 oz (Rich in lean protein and iron)
- **Butter (Grass-fed):** 3 tablespoons (Provides healthy fats and rich flavor)
- **Salt (Himalayan or Sea Salt):** 1/4 teaspoon (Contains essential trace minerals)
- **Black Pepper:** To taste (Enhances flavor)
- **Fresh Thyme:** 1 tablespoon, chopped (Adds aroma and antioxidants)
- **Fresh Rosemary:** 1 tablespoon, chopped (Enhances flavor and nutrients)
- **Garlic Clove:** 1, minced (Adds flavor and beneficial compounds)
- **Olive Oil:** 1 tablespoon (Adds healthy fats and aids grilling)
- **Lemon Zest:** 1/2 teaspoon (Optional for freshness and brightness)

Instructions:

Prepare the Venison Loin:

- Season the venison loin with salt and black pepper on all sides.
- Rub the loin with olive oil, ensuring it is evenly coated.

Grill the Venison Loin:

- Preheat a grill or grill pan to medium-high heat.
- Place the venison loin on the grill and cook for 5-7 minutes on each side for medium-rare, or until your desired level of doneness is reached. Remove from the grill and let it rest for 5 minutes.

Make the Herb Butter:

- In a small saucepan, melt the butter over low heat.
- Add minced garlic, fresh thyme, and rosemary, stirring until the garlic is fragrant.

Serve:

- Slice the grilled venison loin and arrange it on a plate.
- Drizzle with herb butter and garnish with lemon zest if desired.
- Serve immediately for a delicious and nutrient-rich dinner.

Scientific Note:

Venison is a lean game meat rich in protein, iron, and B vitamins, supporting muscle maintenance and energy metabolism. Its lower fat content compared to other red meats makes it an ideal choice for a Ketovore diet.

Butter from grass-fed sources provides healthy fats, including conjugated linoleic acid (CLA) and omega-3 fatty acids, which have anti-inflammatory properties and support heart health.

Herbs like thyme and rosemary offer antioxidants and bioactive compounds that can aid digestion and reduce inflammation, enhancing the flavor and nutritional profile of the dish.

Nutritional Information (per serving):

- Calories: ~650
- Protein: 55g
- Total Fat: 48g
- Saturated Fat: 22g
- Carbohydrates: <1g
- Fiber: 0g

Braised Rabbit with Tarragon Cream Sauce

Serves: 1

Cooking Time: 1 hour

Ingredients and Portions/Measurements:

- **Rabbit Legs:** 2 (Rich in lean protein and essential nutrients)
- **Butter (Grass-fed):** 3 tablespoons (Adds healthy fats and richness)
- **Salt (imalayan or Sea Salt):** 1/4 teaspoon (Contains essential trace minerals)
- **Black Pepper:** To taste (Enhances flavor)
- **Heavy Cream:** 1/4 cup (Adds creaminess and healthy fats)
- **Fresh Tarragon:** 1 tablespoon, chopped (Adds flavor and nutrients)
- **Garlic Cloves:** 2, minced (Adds flavor and beneficial compounds)
- **Dry White Wine:** 1/4 cup (Optional for deglazing and flavor)

Instructions:

Prepare the Rabbit:

- Season the rabbit legs with salt and black pepper on both sides.
- Melt 2 tablespoons of butter in a skillet over medium heat.

Brown the Rabbit:

- Add the rabbit legs to the skillet and brown on all sides for about 5 minutes. Remove from the skillet and set aside.

Make the Tarragon Cream Sauce:

- In the same skillet, add minced garlic and cook until fragrant, about 1 minute.
- Pour in the white wine (if using) and deglaze the pan, scraping up any browned bits.
- Add heavy cream and bring to a simmer. Stir in the remaining butter and fresh tarragon.

Braise the Rabbit:

- Return the rabbit legs to the skillet, cover, and reduce the heat to low.
- Simmer gently for 35-40 minutes until the rabbit is tender and cooked through.

Serve:

- Plate the braised rabbit and spoon the tarragon cream sauce over the top.
- Serve immediately for a flavorful and comforting meal.

Scientific Note:

Rabbit is a lean source of protein, providing essential nutrients such as B vitamins and selenium, which support energy metabolism and antioxidant defense. Its low fat content makes it an excellent choice for a Ketovore diet.

Butter from grass-fed sources offers healthy saturated fats, including CLA and omega-3 fatty acids, which promote heart health and reduce inflammation.

Tarragon is an herb rich in antioxidants and flavor compounds, enhancing the dish's taste while supporting digestion and metabolic health.

Nutritional Information (per serving):

- Calories: ~720
- Protein: 65g
- Total Fat: 50g
- Saturated Fat: 25g
- Carbohydrates: 2g
- Fiber: 0g

Grilled Ostrich Steak with Ghee and Thyme Glaze

Serves: 1

Cooking Time: 25 minutes

Ingredients and Portions/Measurements:

- **Ostrich Steak:** 8 oz (Lean protein, rich in iron and low in fat)
- **Ghee:** 2 tablespoons (Adds healthy fats and a rich, nutty flavor)

- **Salt (Himalayan or Sea Salt):** 1/4 teaspoon (Contains essential trace minerals)
- **Black Pepper:** To taste (Enhances flavor)
- **Fresh Thyme:** 1 tablespoon, chopped (Adds flavor and antioxidants)
- **Garlic Clove:** 1, minced (Adds flavor and beneficial compounds)
- **Lemon Wedges:** For serving (Optional for a fresh contrast)

Instructions:

Prepare the Ostrich Steak:

- Season the ostrich steak with salt and black pepper on both sides.
- Heat 1 tablespoon of ghee in a skillet or grill pan over medium-high heat.

Cook the Ostrich Steak:

- Add the ostrich steak to the hot skillet and sear for 4-5 minutes on each side for medium-rare, or until your desired doneness. Remove from the skillet and let it rest.

Make the Thyme Glaze:

- In the same skillet, melt the remaining ghee over low heat.
- Add minced garlic and fresh thyme, cooking until fragrant, about 1 minute.

Serve:

- Slice the ostrich steak and drizzle with the ghee and thyme glaze.
- Serve with lemon wedges for a fresh contrast.

Scientific Note:

Ostrich is a lean, red meat that provides a high-quality source of protein, iron, and B vitamins, supporting energy production and muscle maintenance. Its lower fat content makes it a suitable choice for a Ketovore diet.

Ghee is a clarified butter that offers healthy saturated fats, supporting energy levels and the absorption of fat-soluble vitamins. It adds a rich flavor to dishes and is ideal for high-heat cooking.

Thyme is an herb rich in antioxidants and anti-inflammatory properties, enhancing flavor while supporting overall health and digestion.

Nutritional Information (per serving):

- Calories: ~550
- Protein: 60g
- Total Fat: 36g
- Saturated Fat: 18g
- Carbohydrates: <1g
- Fiber: 0g

Pan-Seared Alligator Tail with Lemon Herb Butter

Serves: 1

Cooking Time: 30 minutes

Ingredients and Portions/Measurements:

- **Alligator Tail Meat:** 8 oz (Lean protein source, rich in essential nutrients)
- **Butter (Grass-fed):** 3 tablespoons (Adds healthy fats and rich flavor)
- **Salt (Himalayan or Sea Salt):** 1/4 teaspoon (Contains essential trace minerals)
- **Black Pepper:** To taste (Enhances flavor)
- **Fresh Lemon Juice:** 1 tablespoon (Adds brightness and acidity)
- **Fresh Parsley:** 1 tablespoon, chopped (Adds flavor and antioxidants)
- **Garlic Clove:** 1, minced (Adds flavor and beneficial compounds)

- **Olive Oil:** 1 tablespoon (Provides healthy fats and aids in cooking)

Instructions:

Prepare the Alligator Tail:

- Season the alligator tail meat with salt and black pepper on all sides.
- Heat olive oil in a skillet over medium-high heat.

Cook the Alligator Tail:

- Add the alligator tail to the hot skillet and sear for 4-5 minutes on each side until golden brown and cooked through. Remove from the skillet and let it rest.

Make the Lemon Herb Butter:

- In the same skillet, melt the butter over low heat.
- Add minced garlic and cook until fragrant, about 1 minute.
- Stir in fresh lemon juice and chopped parsley, mixing well.

Serve:

- Slice the alligator tail and arrange it on a plate.
- Drizzle with lemon herb butter and serve immediately.

Scientific Note:

Alligator is a lean source of protein that is rich in essential nutrients like vitamin B12, potassium, and omega-3 fatty acids. It is a healthy alternative to traditional meats, offering a unique flavor profile and supporting muscle growth and repair.

Butter provides healthy fats, including conjugated linoleic acid (CLA) and omega-3 fatty acids, which support heart health and reduce inflammation.

Lemon Juice adds a refreshing contrast and provides vitamin C, which supports immune function and antioxidant defense.

Nutritional Information (per serving):

- Calories: ~580
- Protein: 65g
- Total Fat: 38g
- Saturated Fat: 18g
- Carbohydrates: <1g
- Fiber: 0g

Crispy Duck Breast with Bacon-Caper Sauce

Serves: 1

Cooking Time: 45 minutes

Ingredients and Portions/Measurements:

- **Duck Breast:** 8 oz (Rich in healthy fats and protein)
- **Bacon:** 2 slices (Adds flavor and healthy fats)
- **Capers:** 1 tablespoon (Adds tanginess and flavor)
- **Butter (Grass-fed):** 2 tablespoons (Adds richness)
- **Salt (Himalayan or Sea Salt):** 1/4 teaspoon (Contains essential trace minerals)
- **Black Pepper:** To taste (Enhances flavor)
- **Fresh Rosemary:** 1 teaspoon, chopped (Adds aroma and antioxidants)
- **Garlic Clove:** 1, minced (Adds flavor)

Instructions:

Prepare the Duck Breast:

- Score the skin of the duck breast in a crosshatch pattern without cutting into the meat.
- Season both sides with salt and black pepper.

Cook the Duck Breast:

- Place the duck breast skin-side down in a cold skillet. Turn the heat to medium and cook for 6-8 minutes until the skin is crispy and golden brown.
- Flip the duck breast and cook for another 4-5 minutes for medium-rare. Remove from the skillet and let it rest.

Make the Bacon-Caper Sauce:

- In the same skillet, add bacon and cook until crispy. Remove and crumble the bacon.
- Add butter, minced garlic, and chopped rosemary to the skillet, cooking until fragrant.
- Stir in capers and crumbled bacon, mixing well.

Serve:

- Slice the duck breast and arrange it on a plate.

- Drizzle with bacon-caper sauce and serve immediately.

Scientific Note:

Duck Breast provides high-quality protein and healthy fats, including omega-3 and omega-6 fatty acids, which support cardiovascular health and reduce inflammation. The crispy skin adds texture and flavor.

Bacon and Capers add savory and tangy notes to the dish, enhancing the overall flavor profile while providing additional nutrients and healthy fats.

Rosemary is rich in antioxidants and anti-inflammatory compounds, which can support digestion and overall health.

Nutritional Information (per serving):

- Calories: ~750
- Protein: 60g
- Total Fat: 54g
- Saturated Fat: 22g
- Carbohydrates: 1g
- Fiber: 0g

Sous Vide Bison Steak with Thyme and Shallot Butter

Serves: 1

Cooking Time: 2 hours (including sous vide cooking time)

Ingredients and Portions/Measurements:

- **Bison Steak:** 8 oz (Rich in lean protein and essential nutrients)
- **Butter (Grass-fed):** 3 tablespoons (Adds healthy fats and rich flavor)
- **Salt (Himalayan or Sea Salt):** 1/4 teaspoon (Contains essential trace minerals)
- **Black Pepper:** To taste (Enhances flavor)
- **Fresh Thyme:** 1 tablespoon, chopped (Adds aroma and antioxidants)
- **Shallot:** 1 small, minced (Adds flavor and nutrients)
- **Garlic Clove:** 1, minced (Adds flavor)
- **Olive Oil:** 1 tablespoon (For searing)

Instructions:

Prepare the Bison Steak:

- Season the bison steak with salt and black pepper on both sides.
- Place the steak in a vacuum-sealed bag or a zip-lock bag and add 1 tablespoon of butter and half of the chopped thyme.

Sous Vide the Steak:

- Preheat the sous vide water bath to 130°F (54°C) for medium-rare.
- Place the bagged steak in the water bath and cook for 1.5 to 2 hours.

Sear the Steak:

- Remove the steak from the sous vide bag and pat dry with paper towels.
- Heat olive oil in a skillet over high heat.
- Sear the steak for 1-2 minutes on each side until browned. Remove and let it rest.

Make the Thyme and Shallot Butter:

- In the same skillet, melt the remaining butter over low heat.
- Add minced garlic and shallot, cooking until fragrant and softened, about 2 minutes.
- Stir in the remaining fresh thyme.

Serve:

- Slice the bison steak and arrange it on a plate.
- Drizzle with thyme and shallot butter and serve immediately.

Scientific Note:

Bison is a lean source of protein that provides essential nutrients such as iron, zinc, and B vitamins, supporting muscle maintenance and energy production. Its low fat content makes it a healthy option for a Ketovore diet.

Butter from grass-fed sources provides healthy fats, including conjugated linoleic acid (CLA) and omega-3 fatty acids, which support heart health and reduce inflammation.

Thyme and Shallots are rich in antioxidants and anti-inflammatory compounds, enhancing the dish's flavor and nutritional profile.

Nutritional Information (per serving):

- Calories: ~680
- Protein: 58g
- Total Fat: 48g
- Saturated Fat: 22g
- Carbohydrates: 2g
- Fiber: 0g

CHAPTER 6

14 DAYS MEAL PLAN

Day 1

Breakfast (8:00 AM): Savory Beef and Egg Breakfast Bowl

Lunch (12:00 PM): Crispy Duck Breast with Herbed Butter

Snack (3:00 PM): Crispy Chicken Skin Chips with Beef Tallow Aioli

Dinner (6:30 PM): Herb-Crusted Rack of Elk with Garlic Butter Sauce

Day 2

Breakfast (8:00 AM): Pork Belly and Egg Frittata

Lunch (12:00 PM): Bison Ribeye Steak with Bone Marrow Butter

Snack (3:00 PM): Venison Jerky Bites with Liver Pâté

Dinner (6:30 PM): Pan-Seared Swordfish with Anchovy Herb Butter

Day 3

Breakfast (8:00 AM): Cheesy Beef Omelette Roll

Lunch (12:00 PM): Grilled Quail with Creamy Mushroom Sauce

Snack (3:00 PM): Pork Rind Nachos with Duck Fat Guacamole

Dinner (6:30 PM): Wild Boar Chops with Mustard Cream Sauce

Day 4

Breakfast (8:00 AM): Lamb and Egg Breakfast Skillet

Lunch (12:00 PM): Lamb Chop with Anchovy Herb Butter

Snack (3:00 PM): Seared Beef Heart Skewers with Bone Marrow Dip

Dinner (6:30 PM): Roasted Quail with Bacon-Wrapped Asparagus

Day 5

Breakfast (8:00 AM): Chicken Liver Pâté Breakfast Cups

Lunch (12:00 PM): Pan-Seared Pheasant Breast with Sage Brown Butter

Snack (3:00 PM): Crispy Chicken Livers with Lemon Herb Dip

Dinner (6:30 PM): Grilled Venison Loin with Herb Butter

Day 6

Breakfast (8:00 AM): Pork and Egg Breakfast Tacos

Lunch (12:00 PM): Wild Boar Tenderloin with Dijon Mustard Sauce

Snack (3:00 PM): Smoked Duck Breast Bites with Creamy Bacon Dip

Dinner (6:30 PM): Braised Rabbit with Tarragon Cream Sauce

Day 7

Breakfast (8:00 AM): Bacon-Wrapped Scallop Omelette

Lunch (12:00 PM): Kangaroo Steak with Bacon-Wrapped Asparagus

Snack (3:00 PM): Grilled Octopus Skewers with Caper Herb Dip

Dinner (6:30 PM): Grilled Ostrich Steak with Ghee and Thyme Glaze

Day 8

Breakfast (8:00 AM): Venison Sausage and Mushroom Scramble

Lunch (12:00 PM): Pork Belly with Spiced Lamb Sausage

Snack (3:00 PM): Chicharrón with Bone Broth Cheese Dip

Dinner (6:30 PM): Pan-Seared Alligator Tail with Lemon Herb Butter

Day 9

Breakfast (8:00 AM): Duck Confit and Egg Breakfast Hash

Lunch (12:00 PM): Veal Sweetbreads with Herb-Infused Ghee

Snack (3:00 PM): Lamb Meatballs with Creamy Tallow Dip

Dinner (6:30 PM): Crispy Duck Breast with Bacon-Caper Sauce

Day 10

Breakfast (8:00 AM): Smoked Salmon and Avocado Breakfast Boats

Lunch (12:00 PM): Bison Burger with Egg and Hollandaise Sauce

Snack (3:00 PM): Baked Salmon Skin Chips with Dill Cream Dip

Dinner (6:30 PM): Sous Vide Bison Steak with Thyme and Shallot Butter

Day 11

Breakfast (8:00 AM): Cheesy Beef Omelette Roll

Lunch (12:00 PM): Grilled Quail with Creamy Mushroom Sauce

Snack (3:00 PM): Pork Rind Nachos with Duck Fat Guacamole

Dinner (6:30 PM): Wild Boar Chops with Mustard Cream Sauce

Day 12

Breakfast (8:00 AM): Lamb and Egg Breakfast Skillet

Lunch (12:00 PM): Lamb Chop with Anchovy Herb Butter

Snack (3:00 PM): Seared Beef Heart Skewers with Bone Marrow Dip

Dinner (6:30 PM): Roasted Quail with Bacon-Wrapped Asparagus

Day 13

Breakfast (8:00 AM): Chicken Liver Pâté Breakfast Cups

Lunch (12:00 PM): Pan-Seared Pheasant Breast with Sage Brown Butter

Snack (3:00 PM): Crispy Chicken Livers with Lemon Herb Dip

Dinner (6:30 PM): Grilled Venison Loin with Herb Butter

Day 14

Breakfast (8:00 AM): Pork and Egg Breakfast Tacos

Lunch (12:00 PM): Wild Boar Tenderloin with Dijon Mustard Sauce

Snack (3:00 PM): Smoked Duck Breast Bites with Creamy Bacon Dip

Dinner (6:30 PM): Braised Rabbit with Tarragon Cream Sauce

WEEKLY MEAL PLANNER __1__

MONDAY

BREAKFAST _____

LUNCH _____

SNACKS _____

DINNER _____

TUESDAY

BREAKFAST _____

LUNCH _____

SNACKS _____

DINNER _____

WEDNESDAY

BREAKFAST _____

LUNCH _____

SNACKS _____

DINNER _____

THURSDAY

BREAKFAST _____

LUNCH _____

SNACKS _____

DINNER _____

FRIDAY

BREAKFAST _____

LUNCH _____

SNACKS _____

DINNER _____

SATURDAY

BREAKFAST _____

LUNCH _____

SNACKS _____

DINNER _____

SUNDAY

BREAKFAST _____

LUNCH _____

SNACKS _____

DINNER _____

NOTES

_____

_____

_____

_____

WEEKLY MEAL PLANNER <u>2</u>

MONDAY

BREAKFAST _____

LUNCH _____

SNACKS _____

DINNER _____

TUESDAY

BREAKFAST _____

LUNCH _____

SNACKS _____

DINNER _____

WEDNESDAY

BREAKFAST _____

LUNCH _____

SNACKS _____

DINNER _____

THURSDAY

BREAKFAST _____

LUNCH _____

SNACKS _____

DINNER _____

FRIDAY

BREAKFAST _____

LUNCH _____

SNACKS _____

DINNER _____

SATURDAY

BREAKFAST _____

LUNCH _____

SNACKS _____

DINNER _____

SUNDAY

BREAKFAST _____

LUNCH _____

SNACKS _____

DINNER _____

NOTES

_____

_____

_____

_____

Made in United States
Troutdale, OR
10/11/2024

23680131R00042